SPINE POEMS

SPINE POEMS

An Eclectic Collection of Found Verse for Book Lovers

ANNETTE DAUPHIN SIMON

HARPER
DESIGN

An Imprint of HarperCollins Publishers

Bibliophile

You Are a Badass

I Wrote This for You

And for my family, also badass,
and between every line

TITLES BY: Jane Mount / Jen Sincero / Iain S. Thomas

BIBLIOPHILE

YOU ARE A BADASS® SI

I WROTE THIS FOR YOU

CONTENTS

WHEN TWO SPINES ALIGN: A

ukowski *Poetry*

Selected and Edite
Abel Debritto

olds ☀ *ish* Candl

When Two Spines Align:

Poetry

Ish

TITLES BY: Beth Baumert / Charles Bukowski, edited by Abel Debritto / Peter H. Reynolds

PREFACE

I confess: I haunt bookstores. I lurk in libraries. I meander in museums and stalk beloved book spaces, losing time, and myself, in the stacks. I'll never read all I'd like, but I'll give it a try, because books—tangible objects of imagination and wonder—speak to me.

With a book in one hand and a crayon in the other, I have played with words and pictures for as long as I can remember. Advertising and design was a natural fit, and I enjoyed a career as a creative director with respected national clients. An opportunity for our family eventually prompted a move, and I left agency life for freelance work and more time with my kids. I also began to write and illustrate picture books, and in early 2011, I became a bookseller in a storied independent bookshop in Neptune Beach, Florida. One rainy Sunday afternoon, in a lull that followed an especially strong rush of customers and friends, a colleague and I surveyed the resultant disarray. Small stacks seemed to cover every square inch of the shop. Books waited to be gift wrapped, to be mailed, to be returned to the shelves, to be reordered, or to be sorted

for returns. Advance copies from publishers balanced on boxes, pending a spot on the cart. Everywhere, genres mingled together: science fiction mixed with business, histories with mysteries, and so on—and we laughed as we read titles in their random arrangements.

We were punchy, but we'd discovered a game. Not to be outdone by coincidence, we began our own rearrangements. Considering their titles, we pulled one book from here, topped it with another from there. Before we knew it, we'd composed verses to the universe and collaged notes to our pals. Since our constructions of other people's words appeared almost poem-like, we called them "found verses" and cracked ourselves up. Creating these pieces was fun, partly because the combining of words and images to draw a smile or a sigh reminded me of my work in advertising, finding a new way to see the everyday. And partly because, in their various colors and typefaces and textures and weights, the words in the poems resembled Pop Art.

I was hooked. I started bringing my camera to the bookstore to document the ephemera. My colleagues endured poems at every occasion, including the ordering of lunch (*The Hunger Games* by Suzanne Collins) and a favorite sandwich (*I Am Number Four* by Pittacus Lore). I turned some poems into greeting cards and shared a few on social media. By March 2013, my play had become an obsession, and I challenged myself to post more in April in celebration of National Poetry Month.

Of course, I soon learned that found poetry is a recognized form of writing, with roots extending at least as far back as the 1920s art movements Dadaism and Surrealism. One of Dada's founders, Romanian poet Tristan Tzara, wrote directions for composing a poem with words cut out of the newspaper and pulled from a hat. Later, artists and poets like William S. Burroughs, Ezra Pound, T. S. Eliot, and William Carlos Williams also played with chance and juxtaposition, and reordered existing texts to say something new. Contemporary poet George Ella Lyon creates poems from snippets of letters and diaries or overheard conversations. Austin Kleon and Mary Ruefle create found blackout and whiteout poems using newspapers and old books. Kate Baer's 2021 title, *I Hope This Finds You Well*, gathers erasure poems made on her phone from notes from her supporters and detractors, and in 2013, Nina Katchadourian published a book of spine poems, *Sorted Books*. The website of the Found Poetry Review quotes author Annie Dillard: "By entering a found text as a poem, the poet doubles its context. The original meaning remains intact, but now it swings between two poles. The poet adds, or at any rate increases, the element of delight."

The *process* sure is delightful, and I've continued to make spine poems over the years. Books still yammer from the corners of every library and bookstore I have the privilege to visit. They call from my own loaded shelves. One day, my son suggested I might have enough poems for a tangible object of imagination and wonder—here it is. Perhaps you'll hear a title or two or ten calling your name, or feel inspired to create better, smarter spine poems of your own. I confess: I hope you do.

FICTION

- "Dr. Weiss, at forty, knew that her life had been ruined by literature."
  —Anita Brookner, *The Debut*, 1981

- "Too much truth got in the way."
  —Gregory Maguire, *A Wild Winter Swan*, 2020

- The noun "fiction," meaning something created by the imagination, can be traced to the Latin *fictionem-*, *fictiō*, the "action of shaping or molding," from *fingere*, meaning to knead or form out of clay.

- A storyteller could be called a *fictionist*.

Pretending

Here for It

To Tell You the Truth

Sometimes I Lie

TITLES BY: Holly Bourne / R. Eric Thomas / Gilly Macmillan / Alice Feeney

LY BOURNE *Pretending*

C THOMAS **HERE FOR IT**

TO TELL YOU THE TRUTH G MAC

SOMETIMES I LIE ALI FEEN

...ović   An Ordinary Day

NOTHING SPECIAL

ITZMAN   THEM

YOU!

ra Magsamen

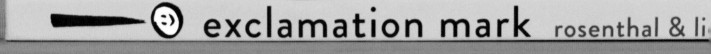
exclamation mark   rosenthal & li...

An Ordinary Day

Nothing Special

Then

You!

Exclamation Mark!

- "It was an ordinary day, a Friday, twenty minutes till lunchtime, five hours till quitting time and the weekend, ten months till vacation, thirty-seven years till retirement. Then the phone rang." —Jack Finney, *Time and Again*, 1970

- "She had understood then that the world—and the space beyond it— was filled with marvel upon marvel, too many marvels to ever count." —Kate DiCamillo, *The Beatryce Prophecy*, illustrated by Sophie Blackall, 2021

- Until it received its own key in 1970, the exclamation mark was made on a typewriter using two keys and three motions—you had to type a period, backspace, and then type an apostrophe above the period.

- In his 1898 collection, *How to Tell a Story, and Other Essays*, Mark Twain cautioned writers against using "whooping exclamation-points." According to the website Quote Investigator, Hollywood journalist Sheilah Graham recounted the time she'd asked F. Scott Fitzgerald for his thoughts on a radio script she had written. In her 1958 memoir, *Beloved Infidel*, she wrote: "'You don't mind if I reword it here and there?' he asked. And though tired from his own writing at the studio, he sat down with a stubby pencil and a pack of cigarettes and painstakingly—and completely—rewrote my copy." Graham continued: "'Cut out all these exclamation points,' he said. 'An exclamation point is like laughing at your own joke.'"

TITLES BY: Elana K. Arnold and Elizabet Vukovic / Geoff Herbach / Morris Gleitzman / Sandra Magsamen / Amy Krouse Rosenthal and Tom Lichtenheld

- "The great flood-gates of the wonder-world swung open."
  —Herman Melville, *Moby-Dick or, the Whale*, 1855

- "It is difficult to know what to do with so much happiness."
  —Naomi Shihab Nye, "So Much Happiness," from *Words Under the Words: Selected Poems*, 1995

- "Stuff your eyes with wonder."
  —Ray Bradbury, *Fahrenheit 451*, 1953

- Brian Selznick's 2011 *Wonderstruck*, a novel in words and pictures about two children who are deaf and born fifty years apart, won the American Library Association's Schneider Family Book Award for excellence in expressing the disability experience. *The Invention of Hugo Cabret* Caldecott Medal winner cited E. L. Konigsburg's 1968 Newbery Medal winner, *From the Mixed-Up Files of Mrs. Basil E. Frankweiler*, among Wonderstruck's inspirations. Selznick also wrote the screenplay for the 2017 movie, which earned Todd Haynes the award for Best Director at the Cannes Film Festival.

Eek!

My Heart

Is Was

Torpedoed

Hundred Percent

Wonderstruck

Didn't See That Coming

Restart

TITLES BY: Julie Larios and Julie Paschkis / Corinna Luyken / Deborah Freedman / Deborah Heiligman / Karen Romano Young / Brian Selznick / Rachel Hollis / Gordon Korman

LARIOS / PASCHKIS   EEK!   5

corinna luyken   my heart   Dial

freedman   is   was   atheneum A

Heiligman   T O R P E D O E D   HENRY HOLT

YOUNG   HUNDRED PERCENT   chronicle books

SELZNICK   WONDER STRUCK   SCHOLASTIC PRESS

DIDN'T SEE THAT COMING   RACHEL HOLLIS   DEY ST.

KORMAN   R E S T A R T

you are · Assell • Copple

THE NIGHT BEFORE CHRISTMAS · M

ooper · THE IRIDESCENCE OF BIRDS

THE WHOLE FROMAGE · KATHE LISON

O'Connor · Wonderland

a book about fonts JUST MY TYPE · SIMON GARFIELD

You Are

The Night Before Christmas

The Iridescence of Birds

The Whole Fromage

Wonderland

Just My Type

- "To me, you will be unique in all the world."
  —Antoine de Saint-Exupéry, *The Little Prince*, 1943

- *Fromage* is the French word for cheese. The phrase "the big cheese" comes from Urdu, in which *chiz* means "a thing." In British India, speakers of English and Urdu called a big thing or event "the real chiz." Now, the expression "the big cheese" is an informal way of referring to an important person.

- Clement Clark Moore wrote "A Visit from St. Nicholas" for his children in 1822, but the poem came to public light when a friend of Moore's sent a copy of it to a local newspaper editor without his permission. The poem was published anonymously in *The Troy (New York) Sentinel* a year later, on December 23, 1823. According to the Library of Congress, Moore didn't claim authorship until 1844.

- Chinese alchemist Pi Sheng invented the first movable type using a mixture of baked clay sometime in the mid-eleventh century. Before then, Chinese artisans created full-length books using hand-carved wooden blocks, a time-consuming and unforgiving process. One wrong move in the carving of the block meant starting the page all over again.

- German Johannes Gutenberg is credited with inventing the printing press in 1439, as well as producing the first book by this method, the Gutenberg Bible.

- The terms "upper case" and "lower case" refer to the physical cases where printers kept their large and small letters. Originally, larger and smaller letters were stored in one case, but eventually the two were divided. Because smaller type was used more often, it was kept in a lower case, where it was easy to reach. The larger letters, used less commonly, were kept in an upper case.

- "She felt the essence of herself pulled finer and smaller like those streams of spun glass that pull and stretch till there remains but a glimmering illusion. Neither falling nor breaking, the stream spins finer. She felt herself very small and ecstatic. Alabama was in love." —Zelda Fitzgerald, *Save Me the Waltz*, 1932

- Rebecca Stead's *When You Reach Me* won the 2010 Newbery Medal for the most outstanding contribution to children's literature. The book was inspired by and had ties to a book that won the 1963 Newbery Medal, Madeline L'Engle's *A Wrinkle in Time*.

- On her website and in her TED Talks, Dr. Helen Fisher, biological anthropologist, senior research fellow at the Kinsey Institute at Indiana University, and author of 2005's *Why We Love: The Nature and Chemistry of Romantic Love*, says humans are wired for love. Brain scans by Fisher and her colleagues show that increased levels of dopamine and oxytocin create feelings of attraction and attachment, while higher levels of testosterone and estrogen tend to shut off the part of the brain that controls rational behavior. Meanwhile, serotonin levels drop, comparable to levels seen in those with obsessive-compulsive disorder. You feel as if, Fisher says, "someone is camping in your head."

What If . . .

When You Reach Me

What If . . . ? Then We . . .

If, Then

I Like It When . . .

What If?

You, Me, We!

This Is My Brain in Love

TITLES BY: Samantha Berger and Mike Curato / Rebecca Stead / Rebecca Kai Dotlich and Fred Koehler / Kate Hope Day / Mary Murphy / Randall Munroe / Erin Jang / I. W. Gregorio

Samantha Berger ✹ Mike Curato ✹ *What If...*

REBECCA STEAD — WHEN *you* REACH *me* — NEWBERY WINNER

DOTLICH · KOEHLER — WHAT IF...? THEN WE... — BOYDS MILLS PRES

IF, THEN — KATE HOPE DAY

Murphy — I Like It When... — RED WAGON PRESCHOOL/HARC

RANDALL MUNROE — what if? —  HMH

2 Fill-in books for parents & kids! — You, Me, We! — ERIN JANG

I. W. GREGORIO — THIS IS MY BRAIN IN LOVE — L B LITTLE, BROWN

Do You Feel Like I Do? Peter Framp

estalten **Do You Read Me?** Books Aroun

Russell Simmons WITH CHRIS MORROW **Do *You!*** 12 LAWS TO ACCESS THE POWER IN *YOU* TO ACHIEVE HAPPINESS AND SUCCESS

ALRIGHT, ALRIGHT, ALRIGHT THE ORAL HISTORY OF RICHARD LINKLATER'S *Dazed and Confused*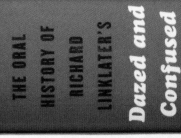

 just checking scenes from the life of an obsessive-compulsive em co

Do You Feel Like I Do?

Do You Read Me?

Do You!

Alright, Alright, Alright

Just Checking

- "If I am out of my mind, it's all right with me, thought Moses Herzog." —Saul Bellow, *Herzog*, 1964

- Maybe you were taught that "alright" is a misspelling of the words "all right." *The American Heritage Guide to Contemporary Usage and Style*, however, says "all right" means "all accurate" or "all correct," while "alright" connotes "sufficient," especially in a less-than-ideal situation.

- In 1946, Delta blues singer Arthur "Big Boy" Crudup wrote the song "That's All Right Mama." Elvis Presley recorded it on July 5, 1954, at Sam Phillips's Sun Records studio in Memphis, Tennessee. Three days later, on July 8, local WHBQ disc jockey Dewey Phillips introduced Elvis to the world when he played the song on his show, *Red, Hot, and Blue*. In a June 27, 1956, interview, Elvis told *The Charlotte Observer*, "I said if I ever got to the place where I could feel all old Arthur felt, I'd be a music man like nobody ever saw."

- In a 2011 interview with Canadian talk show host George Stroumboulopoulos, Matthew McConaughey said a live recording of The Doors' Jim Morrison shouting, "All right!" four times between songs inspired him to use the phrase in the 1993 film *Dazed and Confused*. McConaughey compared Woodson, the character he played, to himself. "I go, 'Man, he's about four things: his car, he's about getting high, he's about rock 'n' roll and picking up chicks.' And I go, 'I'm in my car, I'm high as a kite, I'm listening to rock 'n' roll. . . .' 'Alright, alright, alright.' Three out of four!"

TITLES BY: Peter Frampton with Alan Light / Gestalten, Marianne Julia Strauss, and Jürgen Boos / Russell Simmons with Chris Morrow / Melissa Maerz / Emily Colas

- "Were they not *beguiled* by my adorable outfit? My charming *wit*?"
  —Paul Tobin and Colleen Coover, *Bandette Volume One: Presto!*, 2013

- "'Adorable!' he exclaimed. Then he blew his nose with a loud noise."
  —Victor Hugo, *Les Misérables*, 1862

- "'You flirt with *everything*.' She could tell that her eyes were popping—
  her eyeballs actually felt cold around the edges. 'You flirt with old
  people and babies and everybody in between.'"
  —Rainbow Rowell, *Fangirl*, 2013

- "Some people have a way with words, and other people . . . oh, uh,
  not have way."
  —Steve Martin

- According to Merriam-Webster.com, the word "flirt" was first seen in
  print in 1580. Other words in print for the first time that year include
  "bravado," "comedian," "flaky," and "sweetish."

*Whoa, Dog. Whoa!
What Big Teeth*

Just Joking LOL!

Seriously . . . I'm Kidding

How to Fail at Flirting

TITLES BY: P. D. Eastman / Rose Szabo / National Geographic Kids /
Ellen DeGeneres / Denise Williams

HEZ ... so hard to say ... Simon & Schuster

IN OTHER WORDS ... JHUMPA LAH

Greenwald ... 1 ... TBH, This Is SO Awkward

RIANE DESOMBRE ... I THINK I LOVE YOU ... Underlined

otugno ... You SAY IT First ... B+B

So Hard to Say

In Other Words

TBH, This Is So Awkward

I Think I Love You

You Say It First

- "I know this sounds crazy to say after one encounter but I kind of fell for you pretty hard & it has been forever since I've connected to anyone like this & my heart is kind of broken in a million pieces."
  —B. J. Novak, *One More Thing*, 2014

- "There were some feelings that just didn't have words big enough to describe them."
  —Jodi Picoult, *Between the Lines*, 2012

- In October 2021, Merriam-Webster.com added "TBH" to the dictionary. The abbreviation for "to be honest" is often used in texting and on social media.

- *Mrs. Byrne's Dictionary of Unusual, Obscure, and Preposterous Words* has a few ways to describe nonsensical babble: "baragouin," "gibberish," "glossolalia," and "stultiloquence." To faffle is "to stutter or mumble," to maffle "to mumble or confuse," and a jigamaree is "a word used for lack of a more specific one."

- The mother tongue of Jhumpa Lahiri, author of *In Other Words*, is Bengali. She wrote two novels and two short story collections in English before moving to Rome for three years, where she learned—and wrote her memoir in—Italian. Her first short story collection, *Interpreter of Maladies*, won the Pulitzer Prize and the PEN/Hemingway Award and sold more than 15 million copies worldwide.

- Research says when you can't seem to find a word that's on the tip of your tongue, it's likely not dementia but natural forgetfulness. When words aren't used often, connections are weakened, making retrieval more difficult. The tip-of-the-tongue phenomenon is known as lethologica, and it's universal. Spanish, French, and Italian use the same expression, "at the end of the tongue," to convey it. The German expression *es liegt mir auf der Zunge* means "the word is lying on my tongue," and the Greek phrase *Είναι κάτω από τη γλώσσα μου* (*einai kato apo ti glossa mou*) translates to "it's under my tongue."

TITLES BY: Alex Sanchez / Jhumpa Lahiri / Lisa Greenwald / Auriane Desombre / Katie Cotugno

- "Now this is not the end. It is not even the beginning of the end, but it is, perhaps, the end of the beginning."
—Sir Winston Churchill, in his published collection of war speeches, *The End of the Beginning*, 1943

- "When you realize you want to spend the rest of your life with somebody, you want the rest of your life to start as soon as possible."
—Harry Burns, from Nora Ephron's *When Harry Met Sally*, 1989

- "'Begin at the beginning,' the King said, very gravely, 'and go on till you come to the end: then stop.'"
—Lewis Carroll, *Alice's Adventures in Wonderland*, 1865

- Leonardo da Vinci was renowned for leaving projects unfinished. According to the Uffizi Gallery, Leonardo's first commission was to paint a piece with the Adoration of the Magi as its theme for the main altar in the church of San Donato in Scopeto, a town just outside Florence. Leonardo began *The Adoration of the Magi* in 1481 but abandoned the work in 1482, when he left Florence for the court of Ludovico Sforza, the Regent of Milan. The monks waited for Leonardo to return to Scopeto to finish the work but eventually gave up hope, hiring Filippino Lippi to create a new *Adoration of the Magi* altarpiece in its stead. Lippi completed the painting in 1496.

- In the summer of 1791, musician Count Franz von Walsegg anonymously commissioned an ill Mozart to compose a requiem in memory of his wife. When Mozart died in December 1791, he'd received half the fee but had completed only two movements, leaving sketches for the rest. Mozart's wife, Constanze, worried not only that she might not receive the final payment but that the commissioner would request a refund, turned to composer Joseph von Eybler for help. Eybler orchestrated some of the piece but gave the composition back to Constanze unfinished, with advice to contact one of Mozart's pupils, Franz Xaver Süssmayr. Süssmayr used parts of Eybler's work, added his own, and adapted movements by Mozart, then rewrote the entire piece in his own hand to disguise that it had been written by more than one composer. The Requiem in D Minor was delivered to the count in 1792. It would be a year before Walsegg acknowledged Mozart as the true composer.

Unfinished Business

You Are a Beautiful Beginning

TITLES BY: Vivian Gornick / Nina Laden and Kelsey Garrity-Riley

UNFINISHED BUSINESS VIV

You Are a Beautiful Beginning

Boynton 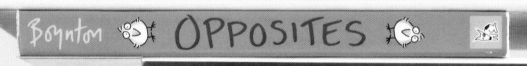 OPPOSITES

on paper THE *EVERYTHING* OF ITS
TWO-THOUSAND-YEAR HISTORY

ER & LUYKEN · nothing in common △

SHUSTERMAN/
SHUSTERMAN DRY

PODOS  like water

VERDE/REYNOLDS * You and Me * ABRAMS ◀

Opposites

On Paper

Nothing in Common

Dry

Like Water

You and Me

- "As different as a moonbeam from lightning, or frost from fire."
  —Emily Brontë, *Wuthering Heights*, 1847

- "What good is warmth without cold to give it sweetness."
  —John Steinbeck, *Travels with Charley: In Search of America*, 1962

- Magnetic attraction, in the scientific sense, involves opposites. Every magnet has both a north and a south pole. The opposite poles attract electron charges to create a stronger pull. Likewise, poles with the same charge repel each other.

- In astrology, opposing sun signs tend to attract each other, not only for their differences, but because there is also a certain characteristic intersection between the two. The six opposing pairings are Aries and Libra, Taurus and Scorpio, Gemini and Sagittarius, Cancer and Capricorn, Leo and Aquarius, and Virgo and Pisces.

- Combining foods that seem to be on opposite ends of the taste spectrum may sound unappealing, but there are those who love the contrast. Americans polled in a 2020 survey commissioned by SPAM and conducted by OnePoll said their favorite odd combo is French fries dipped in a chocolate milkshake. Other top pairings were chocolate and popcorn as well as chocolate with sour cream and onion potato chips. Cookies dipped in guacamole, pickles wrapped in cheese, ice cream on meatloaf, and peanut butter and mayonnaise sandwiches were also choice picks.

TITLES BY: Sandra Boynton / Nicholas A. Basbanes / Kate Hoefler and Corinna Luyken / Neal Shusterman and Jarrod Shusterman / Rebecca Podos / Susan Verde and Peter H. Reynolds

- "I may be heaven-sent, but I'm not perfect."
  —Cynthia Leitich Smith, *Eternal*, 2009

- "It will never be perfect, but perfect is overrated. Perfect is boring."
  —Tina Fey, *Bossypants*, 2011

- Before the toymaker Kohner launched the board game Trouble in 1965, they'd called it Frustration. Trouble is based on an early twentieth-century German game similar to Parcheesi with a name that loosely translates to "Don't Argue." During World War II, brothers Paul and Frank Kohner fled Czechoslovakia to America to escape the Nazis—Paul first, in 1940, and then Frank, in 1942. They formed Kohner Bros. in New York City, manufacturing wooden beaded purses before switching to toys. After World War II, when plastic became available and cheap, Paul Kohner commissioned engineer Albert Stubbmann to convert the toy factory from wood to plastic production. Stubbmann's name is on more than twenty patents for at least fifty products, including the Pop-O-Matic dice device in the center of the Trouble board. Fred Kroll's obituary of August 6, 2003, credits him with the creation of Trouble, as well as the 1970s game Hungry Hungry Hippos. Trouble was eventually acquired by Milton Bradley, which was bought by Hasbro in 1984.

- Erik Larson's history *The Splendid and the Vile: A Saga of Churchill, Family, and Defiance During the Blitz* uses diaries and public records to follow British prime minister Winston Churchill and his advisers through his first year of leadership, during the Nazi World War II bombing campaign from May 1940 through May 1941.

A Crooked Kind of Perfect

A Good Kind of Trouble

A Beautifully Foolish Endeavor

Me with You

The Splendid and the Vile

What's Not to Love

TITLES BY: Linda Urban / Lisa Moore Ramée / Hank Green / Kristy Dempsey and Christopher Denise / Erik Larson / Emily Wibberley and Austin Siegemund-Broka

LINDA URBAN *A Crooked Kind of Perfect* HMH

Ramée A Good Kind of Trouble B+B

A BEAUTIFULLY FOOLISH ENDEAVOR HANK GRE

• Christopher Denise ME WITH YOU Philomel

LARSON THE **SPLENDID** AND THE **VILE** CROWN

EMILY WIBBERLEY
AUSTIN SIEGEMUND-BROKA *What's Not to Love* VIKING

MAN
HDIE

Midnight's Children

N • ROGERS   FOREVER YOUNG

PARKER

VAMPIRES NEVER GET OLD

TALES

Midnight's Children

Forever Young

Vampires Never Get Old

- Salman Rushdie's *Midnight's Children* won the 1981 Booker Prize for best novel of the year; a Booker of Bookers; and in 2008 the Best of the Bookers. His 1988 novel, *The Satanic Verses*, was short-listed for the Booker. Many Muslims considered the book blasphemous, and in 1989, the Ayatollah Khomeini of Iran issued a fatwa calling for Rushdie's death. As of late 2021, Rushdie says there have been no developments for at least five years, though technically the fatwa still stands.

- Bob Dylan wrote "Forever Young" as a lullaby for his son Jesse; the song first appeared on Dylan's 1974 album *Planet Waves*. Dylan won the Nobel Prize for Literature in 2016. In his acceptance speech, more than three months after the ceremony, he cited the influence of Buddy Holly, ragtime blues, Georgia sea shanties, Appalachian ballads, cowboy songs, and three books that had stayed with him since grammar school: *Moby-Dick*, *All Quiet on the Western Front*, and *The Odyssey*. Of the latter, Dylan said, "I return once again to Homer, who says, 'Sing in me, oh Muse, and through me tell the story.'"

- The vampire first appeared in eighteenth-century poetry. The figure became synonymous with Gothic fiction with the 1819 publication of John William Polidori's *The Vampyre*, said to have been inspired by Lord Byron.

- Polidori was Lord Byron's personal physician. In summer 1816, he, along with poet Percy Bysshe Shelley and Shelley's wife, Mary, was a guest at Byron's Lake Geneva villa. Inclement weather kept the foursome indoors; to pass the time, they held a ghost story competition. Eighteen-year-old Mary Shelley's story, *Frankenstein; or, The Modern Prometheus*, became the world's first science fiction novel. When the book was published in 1818, Mary Shelley was twenty.

TITLES BY: Salman Rushdie / Bob Dylan and Paul Rogers / Zoraida Córdova and Natalie C. Parker

- "It seemed like forever ago, like we've had this brief but still infinite forever. Some infinities are bigger than other infinities."
  —John Green, *The Fault in Our Stars*, 2012

- "Look, there. Now. Now. Now."
  —Sarah Dessen, *The Truth About Forever*, 2006

- In Greek mythology, the gods drank ambrosia—said to come from the horn of a magical goat named Amalthea, the foster mother of Zeus—to live forever. The Elixir of Life was delivered daily to the gods by holy doves.

- *The Epic of Gilgamesh* is a tale of the King of Eruk, who after the death of his friend Enkidu undertakes a dangerous journey to discover the secrets of eternal life. The poem is regarded as the earliest surviving literature, written in cuneiform script on twelve clay tablets in Mesopotamia around 3000 BC.

- Although legend has it that sixteenth-century Spanish explorer Juan Ponce de León looked for—and found—the Fountain of Youth in the natural spring in St. Augustine, Florida, many historians now doubt the quest and believe he came ashore instead about 140 miles south, near present-day Melbourne, Florida. Whether or not Ponce de León searched for it, those of us who've tasted the sulfur-smelling water of the fountain grudgingly admit we've seen no turnings of the clock.

- Madame Tussauds says it takes more than twenty artists in excess of eight hundred hours to immortalize a figure in wax. All figures are made about 2 percent larger than the actual subjects, though. Wax shrinks.

A Beginner's Guide to Immortality:

Here We Are

Here We Are

We Are Still Here!

Here to Stay

Here the Whole Time

I Want You to Know We're Still Here

TITLES BY: Maria Birmingham and Josh Holinaty / Kelly Jensen / Oliver Jeffers / Traci Sorell and Frané Lessac / Sara Farizan / Vitor Martins and Larissa Helena / Esther Safran Foer

am · Holinaty | A Beginner's Guide to IMMORTALITY: From Alchemy t

SEN HERE WE ARE

FEMINISM FOR THE REAL WORLD

HERE WE ARE OLI

We Are Still Here!

RIZAN HERE TO STAY

rTINS HERE the WHOLE TIME

I WANT YOU TO KNOW WE'RE STILL HERE ESTHER

REMOTE CONTROL NNED

hD An Outsider's Guide to Humans

Remote Control

An Outsider's Guide to Humans

- "Humans see what they want to see."
  —Rick Riordan, *The Lightning Thief*, 2005

- "You'll know her more by your questions than by her answers."
  —Jerry Spinelli, *Stargirl*, 2000

- The first wireless TV remote control, the Zenith Flash-Matic, was invented by engineer Eugene J. Polley in 1955. It worked like a flashlight and looked like a snub-nosed revolver, a shape chosen so that viewers in the age of TV Westerns might "shoot out" commercials. Zenith sold thirty thousand televisions with the remote control; Polley received a thousand-dollar bonus for his work. Colleague Robert Adler soon developed a more efficient and better-selling device that used sound rather than light, and news accounts often mistakenly described Adler as the remote's sole inventor. In a 2002 interview, eighty-six-year-old Polley said, "The flush toilet may have been the most civilized invention ever devised, but the remote control is the next most important. It's almost as important as sex."

- *The Man Who Fell to Earth*, a 1963 science fiction novel by Walter Tevis, is the story of an extraterrestrial who comes to Earth in search of a way to export water to save his home planet from severe drought. The novel was later made into the 1976 cult classic starring David Bowie as the alien Thomas Jerome Newton. Tevis wrote six novels, including *The Color of Money* and *The Hustler*, which were also made into films.

- Bowie's alter ego, Ziggy Stardust, a glam-rock alien who performed with his band, the Spiders from Mars, made him an international star. Bowie recorded several hits about space including "Starman," "Life on Mars?," "The Prettiest Star," and "Space Oddity." His album *Blackstar* was released on his sixty-ninth birthday, just two days before his death on January 10, 2016.

TITLES BY: Nnedi Okorafor / Camilla Pang

- "Logical but not reasonable. Wasn't that the definition of a robot?"
  —Isaac Asimov, *The Naked Sun*, 1957

- "'You're not a monster,' I said. But I lied."
  —Ocean Vuong, *On Earth We're Briefly Gorgeous*, 2019

- "I have never seen greater monster or miracle in the world than myself."
  —Michel de Montaigne, *The Complete Essays*, Volume 9, 1572

- "I'd rather take coffee than compliments just now."
  —Louisa May Alcott, *Little Women*, 1868

- Coffee didn't become popular in America until 1773, when the Boston Tea Party made switching from tea to coffee a patriotic symbol. Today, New Yorkers are said to drink seven times more coffee than residents of any other U.S. city.

- French writer and philosopher Voltaire was rumored to drink forty to fifty cups of coffee a day. Teddy Roosevelt was said to drink a gallon. Mark Pendergrast, author of *Uncommon Grounds: The History of Coffee and How It Transformed Our World*, says that while Roosevelt is credited with coining the phrase "Good to the last drop" in 1907 when he'd had a cup after touring Andrew Jackson's former home, the Hermitage, stories vary as to Roosevelt's exact words, and even which brand of coffee he drank. Nonetheless, the headline in one 1920s ad for Maxwell House coffee and its marketers, the Cheek-Neal Coffee Company of Houston, Texas, proclaimed: "Teddy Roosevelt Gave Popular Slogan to Maxwell House Coffee."

Robot Zombie Frankenstein!

Once I Was You

Once Upon a Time This Morning

Before

Coffee

TITLES BY: Annette Simon / Maria Hinojosa / Anne Rockwell and Susie Stevenson / Anna Todd / H. E. Jacob

ROBOT ZOMBIE FRANKENSTEIN!

Once I Was You

M

nson Once Upon a Time This Morning

BEFORE ∞

A

COFFEE

THE EPIC O
COMMODI

POETRY

OLLINS The Trouble with Poetry

NOTHING RHYMES WITH ORANGE

The Trouble with Poetry

Nothing Rhymes with Orange

- "Only the very weak-minded refuse to be influenced by literature and poetry."
  —Cassandra Clare, *Clockwork Angel*, 2010

- "Poetry is not only dream and vision, it is the skeleton architecture of our lives."
  —Audre Lorde, "Poetry Is Not a Luxury," from *Sister Outsider: Essays and Speeches*, 1984

- Poetry comes from the Greek word *poesis*, meaning "making" or "creating."

- David Scott Kastan and Stephen Farthing, authors of Yale University's 2018 *On Color*, say that while Chaucer described it as a "color betwixe yelow and reed," the English word for the color orange occurred only when the fruit became common in Europe, sometime in the seventeenth century.

- Alice Walker's first book of poetry, *Once*, was published in 1968 when she was twenty-four years old. Fifteen years later, she won the Pulitzer Prize for her third novel, *The Color Purple*.

- Other English words that have no rhyme include the colors "purple" and "silver."

TITLES BY: Billy Collins / Adam Rex

- "We hear poetry from the moment we are conceived. Our mothers sing songs to us in the womb while they smile and anticipate." —Nikki Giovanni, "Lemonade Grows from Soil, Too," from *Make Me Rain*, 2021

- "When you're talking about a marrow experience—like an experience that touches your bone marrow—you want to use the strongest platform you can, and for me, that was poetry." —Laurie Halse Anderson, on *Shout*, her 2019 novel written in verse, in conversation with NPR's Melissa Block

- In 1996, to champion poets and poetry in our culture and to make poetry more accessible to the public, the Academy of American Poets designated April as National Poetry Month. According to their website, the academy offers activities and resources for millions of readers, students, librarians, and booksellers, including podcasts, festivals, and workshops, making it "the largest literary celebration in the world." Poem in Your Pocket Day began in New York City in 2002 with the Office of the Mayor and the city's Departments of Cultural Affairs and Education. In 2008, the academy expanded Poem in Your Pocket Day across the United States, and in 2016, the League of Canadian Poets brought the day's specific celebration to Canada.

- Within hours of reading her poem "The Hill We Climb" at the 2021 inaugurations of Joe Biden and Kamala Harris, twenty-two-year-old National Youth Poet Amanda Gorman saw two not-yet-published books top Amazon's bestseller lists. Initially titled *The Hill We Climb and Other Poems*, *Call Us What We Carry* became the first book of poetry to debut at number one on *USA Today*'s Best-Selling Books list and the first book of poetry to claim that spot since the list started in 1993.

A Little History of Poetry

Your Voice in My Head

Floating in a Most Peculiar Way

TITLES BY: John Carey / Emma Forrest / Louis Chude-Sokei

N CAREY   A LITTLE HISTORY OF POETRY

YOUR VOICE IN MY HEAD   EMMA F

FLOATING IN A MOST PECULIAR WAY   LO

The **World Between Two Covers**

WHAT WE SEE WHEN WE READ PET

The World Between Two Covers
What We See When We Read

- "Perhaps travel cannot prevent bigotry, but by demonstrating that all peoples cry, laugh, eat, worry, and die, it can introduce the idea that if we try to understand each other, we may even become friends."
—Maya Angelou, "Passports to Understanding," *Wouldn't Take Nothing for My Journey Now*, 1993

- " 'My grandfather always says that's what books are for,' Ashoke said, using the opportunity to open the volume in his hands. 'To travel without moving an inch.' "
—Jhumpa Lahiri, *The Namesake*, 2003

- "I was surprised, as always, by how easy the act of leaving was, and how good it felt. The world was suddenly rich with possibility."
—Jack Kerouac, *On the Road*, 1955

- "The whole world is full of things and there's a crying need for someone to find them."
—Astrid Lindgren, *Pippi Longstocking*, 1950

- The term "bookworm" was originally considered an insult. The Elizabethan put-down for a person of contempt was "worm," and a "bookworm" referred to a person who read too much.

- The origin of the idiom "Don't judge a book by its cover" is unclear. Mr. Tulliver, a character in George Eliot's 1860 novel *The Mill on the Floss*, defends his young daughter's reading of Daniel Defoe's *The Political History of the Devil* with, "But they've all got the same covers, and I thought they were all o' one sample, as you may say. But it seems one mustn't judge by th' outside." An 1867 article in the newspaper *The Piqua Democrat* about a championship baseball game between the favored Piqua, Ohio, Sterlings, and the Port Jefferson Defiance ends: "MORAL. Don't judge a book by its cover, nor a man by his cloth, as there is often a good deal of solid worth and superior skill underneath a linsey jacket and yaller pants." Several sources trace a version either to a 1929 or 1944 edition of the journal *American Speech* as "You can't judge a book by its binding," or to 1946 mystery *Murder in the Glass Room* by Edwin Rolfe and Lester Fuller, which reads, "You can never tell a book by its cover."

- "I lie to myself all the time. But I never believe me."
  —S. E. Hinton, *The Outsiders*, 1967

- "Things come apart so easily when they have been held together with lies."
  —Dorothy Allison, *Bastard out of Carolina*, 1992

- "Lies require commitment."
  —Veronica Roth, *Divergent*, 2011

- Honey, food of the gods, has long been considered an aphrodisiac. Legend has it that Cupid, child of the goddess Venus, dipped his arrows in honey before aiming at the imminent lovestruck.

- Saint Valentine, the patron saint of romance, is also the patron saint of beekeeping.

- The origin of the candy conversation hearts known as Sweethearts goes back to 1847, when Boston pharmacist Oliver Chase invented a machine to cut medicinal lozenges for sore throats. High demand for the lozenges without medicine—as clove- or cinnamon-flavored candies—led Chase to create what would become America's longest-operating candy company, the New England Confectionery Company, or NECCO. In 1866, Oliver's brother, Daniel, devised a way to press words on the candies with a felt roller and vegetable coloring, usually red. These "conversation candies" took on their heart shape in 1902. NECCO was bought by Spangler Candy in 2018, and after a two-year absence from the shelves, Sweethearts returned in 2020.

Honey, Baby, Sweetheart

We Were Liars

Tell Me More

TITLES BY: Deb Caletti / E. Lockhart / Kelly Corrigan

Honey, Baby, Sweetheart CALETTI

art we were liars

Tell Me More KELLY C

LLO ~ KIM   *La La La*   CANDLEWICK

Lulu Delacre   Turning Pages

Before the coffee gets cold
HANOVER SQUARE PRESS

Happy PEOPLE READ & *Drink* COFFEE   AGN

LLO ~ KIM   *La La La*   CANDLEWICK

La La La

Turning Pages

Before the Coffee Gets Cold

Happy People Read & Drink Coffee

La La La

- "It is well known that reading quickens the growth of a heart like nothing else."
  —Catherynne M. Valente, *The Girl Who Circumnavigated Fairyland in a Ship of Her Own Making*, 2012

- "She read books as one would breathe air, to fill up and live."
  —Annie Dillard, *The Living*, 1992

- "Books are a uniquely portable magic."
  —Stephen King, *On Writing*, 2000

- Reading makes us happier. In a 2015 article in *The New Yorker*, Ceridwen Dovey says reading "has been shown to put our brains into a pleasurable trance-like state, similar to meditation, and it brings the same health benefits of deep relaxation and inner calm." Research from the University of Sussex shows just six minutes of reading can reduce stress by 68 percent.

- Coffee drinking makes us happier too. Studies show the caffeine in coffee increases levels of dopamine in our brains, prompting feelings of pleasure and euphoria similar to those caused by cocaine and marijuana. Dr. Gary L. Wenk, professor of psychology and neuroscience at The Ohio State University and author of *Your Brain on Food: How Chemicals Control Your Thoughts and Feelings*, says, "Coffee makes us feel so good because it is able to tap into virtually every reward system our brain has evolved."

TITLES BY: Kate DiCamillo and Jaime Kim / Sonia Sotomayor and Lulu Delacre / Toshikazu Kawaguchi / Agnès Martin-Lugand / Kate DiCamillo and Jaime Kim

NONFICTION

WHAT IT IS

LYNDA

WHAT TO EXPECT 5TH EDITION **WHEN YOU'RE EXPECTING**

SOMETHING ELSE

KA

What It Is

What to Expect When You're Expecting

Something Else

- "Mrs. Lynde says, 'Blessed are they who expect nothing for they shall not be disappointed.' But I think it would be worse to expect nothing than to be disappointed."
  —L. M. Montgomery, *Anne of Green Gables*, 1908

- "Expect everything so that nothing comes unexpected."
  —Norton Juster, *The Phantom Tollbooth*, 1961

- "One always expects something else."
  —Erich Maria Remarque, *Arch of Triumph: A Novel of a Man Without a Country*, 1945

- In a 2006 post for the *New York Times*, William Safire wrote that the phrase "It is what it is" appeared as early as 1949, in a column by J. E. Lawrence in the *Nebraska State Journal* about the hardscrabble life there. " 'New land is harsh, and vigorous, and sturdy. . . . There is nothing of sham or hypocrisy in it. It is what it is, without apology.' "

TITLES BY: Lynda Barry / Heidi Murkoff / Kathryn Cave and Chris Riddell

- "You can't depend on your eyes when your imagination is out of focus." —Mark Twain, *A Connecticut Yankee in King Arthur's Court*, 1889

- "Truth is a matter of the imagination." —Ursula K. Le Guin, *The Left Hand of Darkness*, 1969

- "Our imagination is our greatest hope for survival." —Keith Haring, *Keith Haring Journals*, 2010

- The son of migrant farm workers, Juan Felipe Herrera, author of *Imagine*, taught himself to read and write English as a child. In 2012, he was named California's poet laureate, and in 2015, the poet laureate of the United States.

- John Lennon said his song "Imagine," from the 1971 album of the same name, was inspired by several poems from wife Yoko Ono's 1964 book, *Grapefruit*. One poem, titled "Cloud Piece," reads: "Imagine the clouds dropping. Dig a hole in your garden to put them in." The poem was eventually reproduced on the album's back cover.

- In a 1980 BBC interview quoted in the 2018 book *Imagine John Yoko* by John Lennon and Yoko Ono, Lennon said "Imagine" should have been credited as a Lennon/Ono song, "but those days I was a bit more selfish, a bit more macho, and I sort of omitted her contribution." Twenty-one years after the song's debut, the National Music Publishers' Association announced that Yoko Ono would be added as a songwriter.

- Before he wrote his number one *New York Times* bestselling *Tale of Magic* series, Chris Colfer won a 2010 Golden Globe and was named to the 2011 TIME 100, *Time* magazine's listing of the most influential people in the world, for his portrayal of Kurt Hummel on the musical TV series *Glee*. The show ran from 2009 to 2015 and won six Emmys. Fans referred to themselves as "Gleeks."

Imagine

A Tale of Magic . . .

It Looks Like This

TITLES BY: Juan Felipe Herrera and Lauren Castillo / Chris Colfer / Rafi Mittlefehldt

imagine

A Tale of Magic...

LB LITTLE, BROWN

It Looks Like This

Art =

ANSWERS IN THE FORM OF QUESTIONS
A DEFINITIVE HISTORY AND INSIDER'S GUIDE TO *JEOPARDY!*

I SAY OOH YOU SAY AAH

Art =

Answers in the Form of Questions

I Say Ooh You Say Aah

- "All art is at once surface and symbol. Those who go beneath the surface do so at their peril."
  —Oscar Wilde, *The Picture of Dorian Gray*, 1890

- "All art is a kind of confession, more or less oblique."
  —James Baldwin, *Nobody Knows My Name: More Notes of a Native Son*, 1961

- "Once introduced into society, the work of art begins to pulsate with those meanings, emotions, ideas brought to it by its audience and over which the artist has but limited control."
  —Ralph Ellison, *Shadow and Act*, 1964

- "Not everyone can be the artist. There have to be those who witness the art, who love and appreciate what they have been privileged to see."
  —Ann Patchett, *Bel Canto*, 2001

- "If a painting really works down in your heart and changes the way you see, and think, and feel, you don't think, 'oh, I love this picture because it's universal.' 'I love this painting because it speaks to all mankind.' That's not the reason anyone loves a piece of art. It's a secret whisper from an alleyway. *Psst, you. Hey kid. Yes you.*"
  —Donna Tartt, *The Goldfinch*, 2013

TITLES BY: The Metropolitan Museum of Art / Claire McNear / John Kane

- "PAY ATTENTION TO WHAT YOU PAY ATTENTION TO."
—Amy Krouse Rosenthal, @missamykr, March 15, 2013

- "Such as, for example: a gaggle of children trudging through a side-blown December flurry; a friendly match-share beneath some collision-tilted streetlight; a frozen clock, bird-visited within its high tower; cold water from a tin jug; toweling off one's clinging shirt post–June rain. Pearls, rags, buttons, rug-tuft, beer-froth. Someone's kind wishes for you; someone remembering to write; someone noticing that you are not at all at ease."
—George Saunders, *Lincoln in the Bardo*, 2017

- "She was like that, excited and delighted by little things, crossing her fingers before any remotely unpredictable event, like tasting a new flavor of ice cream, or dropping a letter in a mailbox."
—Jhumpa Lahiri, *Interpreter of Maladies*, 1999

- Cheryl Strayed wrote the essays in *Tiny Beautiful Things* as an unpaid advice columnist for the online literary magazine *The Rumpus*, under the pseudonym "Sugar." When she stopped writing the column in 2012, she revealed her identity as the author of the bestselling memoir *Wild: From Lost to Found on the Pacific Crest Trail*. While hiking the Pacific Crest Trail, Strayed brought along "an old friend," Adrienne Rich's *The Dream of a Common Language*.

The Whisper

The Egg

The Watermelon Seed

The Art of the Commonplace

Tiny Beautiful Things

TITLES BY: Pamela Zagarenski / Geraldo Valério / Greg Pizzoli / Wendell Berry / Cheryl Strayed

THE WHISPER

THE **EGG** Owl kids

THE WATERMELON SEED

the art of the commonplace
THE AGRARIAN ESSAYS OF Wendell Berry

tiny beautiful things   Advice on love and li
from Dear Sugar

The Art of Talking to Yourself

This Just Speaks to Me

The Art of Theft

Double Take!

TITLES BY: Vironika Tugaleva / Hoda Kotb

TITLES BY: Sherry Thomas / Susan Hood and Jay Fleck

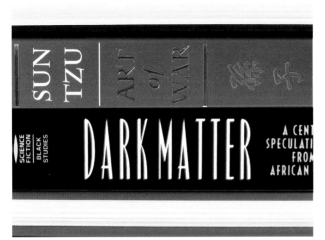

Art of War

Dark Matter

The Art of Wishing

I Really Needed This Today

TITLES BY: Sun Tzu / Sheree R. Thomas

TITLES BY: Lindsay Ribar / Hoda Kotb

- "In the history of art there are periods when bread seems so beautiful that it nearly gets into museums."
  —Janet Flanner, *Paris Was Yesterday, 1925–1939*, 1972

- "The heat of the bread burned into my skin, but I clutched it tighter, clinging to life."
  —Suzanne Collins, *The Hunger Games*, 2008

- "In one life she only ate toast."
  —Matt Haig, *The Midnight Library*, 2020

- The most famous literary breadcrumbs might be those left in a trail for Hansel and Gretel in 1812's *Grimm's Fairy Tales*. Jacob and Wilhelm Grimm credited "various tales from Hesse" as their source for the story, though some believe they first heard parts of it from the family of Wilhelm's friend and future wife, Dortchen Wild.

- Marie-Catherine Le Jumel de Barneville, the French Comtesse d'Aulnoy, coined the term "fairy tale" in 1697–1698 with the publication of her first collection, *Les Contes de Fées, I–III*. Madame d'Aulnoy often tested her tales at her popular literary salon, where like minds could gather away from King Louis XIV and his court. Fairy tales became a way to critique the French court without openly doing so.

- The most famous literary cookie crumbs may be those of Proust's madeleine in his 1907 novel, *À La Recherche du Temps Perdu*, or *In Search of Lost Time*. In 2015, Paris publishing house Saint-Pères revealed earlier versions handwritten by Proust. The madeleine showed up only in the third draft. In the second, Proust had written instead of a biscotte. And in the first draft? Toasted bread.

Still Life with Bread Crumbs

Another Day

Already Toast

TITLES BY: Anna Quindlen / David Levithan / Kate Washington

NNA QUINDLEN STILL LIFE WITH BREAD CRUMBS

 another day

ON ALREADY TOAST
CAREGIVING AND BURNOUT IN AMERICA

N BECKER **MY FAVORITE COLOR** CANDLEWICK

H Y S T E R I A

My Favorite Color

Hysteria

- "With the very first rays of light it came alive in me: hope. As things emerged in outline and filled with color, hope increased until it was like a song in my heart."
—Yann Martel, *Life of Pi*, 2001

- "If there are words for all the pastels in a hue—the lavenders, mauves, fuchsias, plums, and lilacs—who will name the tones and tints of a smell?"
—Diane Ackerman, *A Natural History of the Senses*, 1990

- A 2015 YouGovAmerica survey said blue was the most popular color in Britain, Germany, the United States, Australia, China, Hong Kong, Malaysia, Singapore, Thailand, and Indonesia.

- German scientist Kai Kupferschmidt, author of the 2021 title *Blue: In Search of Nature's Rarest Color*, says few living things are naturally blue. Many only appear so because of how our brains perceive light. Of cornflowers, which don't absorb any blue light, he writes, "In a sense, blue is what the plant rejects. Calling it blue is a bit like calling a country club 'feminist' because it doesn't allow women."

- The word "hysteria" is said to have come from the Greek adjective *hysterikos*, "coming from the womb," coined by Hippocrates in his *Sicknesses of Women* to refer to the physical conditions of a "wandering womb." In 1878, Jean-Martin Charcot, the founder of modern neurology as well as Sigmund Freud's mentor, claimed not only that hysteria was a female disease, but that the ability to be hypnotized was a clinical, identifying factor. In their 2019 book, *How the Brain Lost Its Mind: Sex, Hysteria, and the Riddle of Mental Illness*, Dr. Allan H. Ropper and Brian David Burrell wrote about Charcot's response to increasing pressure from the research community: "Toward the end, even Charcot had privately begun to acknowledge his mistake. *Le grand hypnotisme*, he conceded, was not a true disorder or even a syndrome. . . . He also backed down from his claims about hysteria as a disease of the body, at least in private."

TITLES BY: Aaron Becker / Jessica Gross

- "If you surrendered to the air, you could *ride* it."
  —Toni Morrison, *Song of Solomon*, 1977

- "But still, like air, I'll rise."
  —Maya Angelou, "Still I Rise," *And Still I Rise: A Book of Poems*, 1978

- "I am no bird; and no net ensnares me."
  —Charlotte Brontë, *Jane Eyre*, 1847

- "It was all about letting go of everything."
  —Pema Chödrön, *When Things Fall Apart: Heart Advice for Difficult Times*, 1996

- "Un-," a prefix of negation, is the most prolific of English prefixes, forming more than one thousand compounds. It is often used euphemistically, for example, making an "untruth" more polite than a "lie." "Un-" had its moment in the lemon-limelight in ads for 7-Up that began in 1968, when agency J. Walter Thompson branded the soft drink as the youthful alternative to "the Establishment" Coke and Pepsi. The Uncola campaign broke racial barriers within the Seven-Up Company, with Trinidadian Geoffrey Holder as the first Black actor in its TV spots.

- Iona and Peter Opie wrote in their 1951 *The Oxford Dictionary of Nursery Rhymes* that "Humpty Dumpty," the egg who fell off a wall and couldn't be put back together again, is so old the rhyme's age could be "measured in thousands of years, or rather it is so great that it cannot be measured at all." The rhyme's origins remain scrambled. One theory says Humpty alludes to King Richard III, who died after a fall from his horse, named "Wall," during the 1485 Battle of Bosworth. Another claims Humpty was a cannon in either Colchester or Gloucester, England, that fell from its place atop the church of the walled town during a siege in 1648, even as this story has been attributed to a spoof in the *Oxford Magazine* in 1956. The *Oxford English Dictionary* says "Humpty-Dumpty" was a seventeenth-century drink of brandy boiled with ale. Literary references to Humpty include *All the King's Men* by Robert Penn Warren, *All the President's Men* by Bob Woodward and Carl Bernstein, and, of course, Lewis Carroll's 1871 *Through the Looking-Glass*.

After the Wreck, I Picked Myself Up, Spread My Wings, and Flew Away

Unbroken

Undaunted

Untamed

TITLES BY: Joyce Carol Oates / Laura Hillenbrand / John O. Brennan / Glennon Doyle

Oates · After the WRECK, I PICKED MYSELF UP, Spread My WINGS, and FLEW Away · FIC OAT · HARPER TEEN

UNBROKEN · LAURA HILLENBR

UNDAUNTED · JO BR

UNTAMED GLENNON

A HISTORY OF MY BRIEF BODY BELCOU

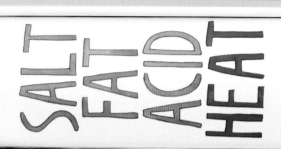SALT FAT ACID HEAT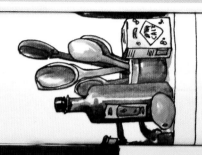

BRAIN ON FIRE SUSA CAHA

L'ENGLE A Wrinkle in Time

Barner Dinosaur Bones chronicle boo

NEGOTIATIONS DESTINY O. BIRDSON

LEAVE OUT THE TRAGIC PARTS DA KIND

A History of My Brief Body

Salt Fat Acid Heat

Brain on Fire

A Wrinkle in Time

Dinosaur Bones

Negotiations

Leave Out the Tragic Parts

- "I've finally recognized my body for what it is: a personality-delivery system, designed expressly to carry my character from place to place, now and in the years to come."
  —Anna Quindlen, *Lots of Candles, Plenty of Cake*, 2012

- Madeleine L'Engle's *A Wrinkle in Time* was rejected by twenty-six publishers who'd claimed it was too difficult and detailed for children before Farrar, Straus and Giroux published it in 1962. In 1963, the book won the Newbery Medal for Distinguished Literature for Children.

- *A Wrinkle in Time* begins "It was a dark and stormy night," as does every novel typed by the character Snoopy in Charles Schulz's *Peanuts* comic strip. Both L'Engle and Schulz chose the opening sentence from the 1830 novel *Paul Clifford* by Edward Bulwer-Lytton because the phrase exemplified bad writing.

- The line is commemorated annually in the Bulwer-Lytton Fiction Contest for the worst first sentence of a nonexistent novel. According to the contest's website, founder Dr. Scott Rice later learned that "the line had been around for donkey's years before Lytton decided to have fun with it but the damage had been done . . . and rendered [Bulwer-Lytton's] name synonymous with bad writing, an author more widely read in his time than Charles Dickens."

- Charles Dickens was Bulwer-Lytton's editor and friend. He named one of his sons, Edward Bulwer Lytton Dickens, after him.

- Bulwer-Lytton is also credited with the phrase "The pen is mightier than the sword," a line spoken by Cardinal Richelieu in Bulwer-Lytton's 1839 play *Richelieu: Or, The Conspiracy, A Play in Five Acts*. The cleric discovers there are plans to murder him, but is unable to respond with violent measures because of his calling.

- "Tomorrow is a new day with no mistakes in it yet."
—L. M. Montgomery, *Anne of Green Gables*, 1908

- "I can't seem to be a pessimist long enough to overlook the possibility of things being overwhelmingly good."
—John Corey Whaley, *Where Things Come Back*, 2011

- "Just because I cannot see it doesn't mean I can't believe it."
—Jack Skellington, in Tim Burton's *The Nightmare Before Christmas*, 1993

- "I'm a glass-is-half-full person now, and your sorry ass is still in half-empty country."
—Janet Evanovich, *Plum Spooky*, 2009

- A person who is optimistic regardless of the circumstances is Panglossian, after a character in Voltaire's 1759 *Candide*. From the Greek *panglossia*, meaning "talkativeness," Dr. Pangloss believes that no matter what happens—sickness, suffering, shipwreck, earthquake, or murder—"everything is for the best." An extreme pessimist is a Chicken Licken (also known as Chicken Little or Henny Penny), after the hen in a children's folktale who, when hit by an acorn, believes the sky is falling.

- When asked if the research for his book *A Short History of Nearly Everything*, which explores the history of science in layperson's terms, made him an optimist or a pessimist, Bill Bryson said, "I don't know. It's hard not to be kind of pessimistic about human beings generally, because we do tend to mess things up. . . . But being a pessimist is just such a gloomy way of looking at things, so I have to hope for the best."

- Again, but better? The film *The Shining*, based on the book by Stephen King and directed by Stanley Kubrick, holds two Guinness World Records for most retakes of a single scene with dialogue. The stair scene with actor Shelley Duvall took 127 shots, but the "shine" discussion between Dick Hallorann and Danny Torrance, played respectively by Scatman Crothers and Danny Lloyd, took 148.

The Optimist

This Time Will Be Different

This Time Next Year

We'll Be Laughing

Again, but Better

TITLES BY: Sophie Kipner / Misa Sugiura / Jacqueline Winspear / Christine Riccio

THE OPTIMIST  SOP
KIPN
102

THIS TIME WILL BE DIFFERENT SUGIURA HARPER TEEN

THIS TIME NEXT YEAR Jacqueline
WE'LL BE LAUGHING Winspear

Again, but Better CHRISTINE
RICCIO

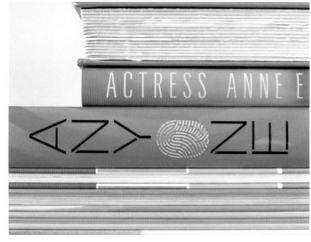

The Archer

Almost Missed You

Actress

Anyone

TITLES BY: Paulo Coelho / Jessica Strawser

TITLES BY: Anne Enright / Charles Soule

The Art Forger

Too Good to Be True

The Abstainer

Not I

TITLES BY: B. A. Shapiro / Carola Lovering

TITLES BY: Ian McGuire / Joachim C. Fest

- "But then, liars do make the best magicians, and he happened to be exceptional."
  —Lisa Maxwell, *The Last Magician*, 2017

- "Perhaps priest and magician were once one, but the priest, learning humility in the face of God, discarded the spell for prayer."
  —Patti Smith, *Just Kids*, 2010

- "What the eyes see and the ears hear the mind believes. I rarely believe a full hundred per cent the explanations I hear or read."
  —Harry Houdini, *A Magician Among the Spirits*, 1924

- Named Erik Weisz at birth in Budapest in 1874, magician and escape artist Harry Houdini chose his stage name in honor of French magician Jean Eugène Robert-Houdin, who is known as the father of modern magic. In 1908, however, Houdini published *The Unmasking of Robert-Houdin*, disparaging the magician and accusing him of stealing tricks from other showmen.

- Not content solely with disappearing tricks, *The Magician's Own Book, or The Whole Art of Conjuring*, published by Dick & Fitzgerald in 1862 described itself as a "Complete Hand-Book of Parlor Magic;" "Containing over One Thousand Optical, Chemical, Mechanical, Magnetical, and Magical Experiments, Amusing Transmutations, Astonishing Sleights and Subtleties, Celebrated Card Deceptions, Ingenious Tricks with Numbers, Curious and Entertaining Puzzles, Together with All the Most Noted Tricks of Modern Performers," "Intended as a Source of Amusement for One Thousand and One Evenings."

- Janis Joplin sang "Piece of My Heart," her biggest chart success, as part of her encore at Woodstock in 1969. Melissa Etheridge sang her own version at Woodstock '94 as part of a four-song medley of Joplin tunes. Clive Davis, the legendary record executive who nurtured the careers of Whitney Houston and Alicia Keys, said he pursued Joplin after hearing her perform at the 1967 Monterey Pop Festival. Joplin's band, Big Brother and the Holding Company, was the first band he signed, to Columbia Records.

The Magician

Son of a Trickster

Piece of My Heart

Disappeared

TITLES BY: W. Somerset Maugham / Eden Robinson / Mary Higgins Clark and Alafair Burke / Francisco X. Stork

SOMERSET MAUGHAM *The Magician* PENGUIN CL

NSON SON OF A TRiCKSTER VINTAGE CANADA

S CLARK SIMON & SCHUSTER PIECE OF MY HEART

KE

RK DISAPPEARED

thel · Jennings · McNicholas **I Am Jazz** Dial

BUSTARD *blue skies* SIMON & SCHUSTER

BIRDSONG GREYS

E MORA SATURDAY

SOLUTIONS and other PROBLEMS Allie B

BOBO **I AM ENOUGH**

I Am Jazz

Blue Skies

Birdsong

Saturday

Solutions and Other Problems

I Am Enough

- "Ninety percent of who you are is invisible."
  —E. L. Konigsburg, *The Mysterious Edge of the Heroic World*, 2007

- "Everyone has an identity. One of their own, and one for show."
  —Jacqueline Susann, *Valley of the Dolls*, 1966

- "'I am not who I was,' he whispered, gripping the edges of the column, 'but I know who I am.'"
  —Christopher Paolini, *Inheritance*, 2011

- *I Am Jazz*, a picture book by a transgender girl published in 2014, has been on the American Library Association's Top 10 Most Challenged Books List nearly every year since. Other titles often banned or challenged include *The Handmaid's Tale* by Margaret Atwood; *The Bluest Eye* by Toni Morrison; *The Hate U Give* by Angie Thomas; *Drama* by Raina Telgemeier; *And Tango Makes Three* by Justin Richardson, Peter Parnell, and Henry Cole; and *Captain Underpants* by Dav Pilkey. Banned Books Week, since 1982 the annual celebration of the freedom to read, is typically held the last week of September.

- The bluebird is the most universally accepted symbol of happiness, prosperity, protection, and renewal in Indigenous cultures worldwide.

- The Romans named Saturday (*Sāturnī diēs*, or Saturn's Day) after the planet Saturn, which was named after the Roman planet *Sāturnus*, which was named after the god Saturn, who was associated with agriculture, fertility, strength, wealth, feasts, and abundance. In ancient times, festivities often took place on Saturn's Day.

TITLES BY: Jessica Herthel, Jazz Jennings, and Shelagh McNicholas / Anne Bustard / Julie Flett / Oge Mora / Allie Brosh / Grace Byers and Keturah A. Bobo

- "[They] would help me write, as cats do, by climbing on to the keyboard."
  —Margaret Atwood, in the introduction to *On Cats: An Anthology*, 2021

- "If cats understood technology and had opposable thumbs, they'd rule the world."
  —P. C. Cast, *Awakened*, 2011

- "We can scold our cats (not that it ever does anyone any good), laugh at our cats, play with them, find faults with them, and be exasperated by their unpredictable moods. The only thing we cannot do is to live without them."
  —Michael Joseph, *Best Cat Stories*, 1952

- T. S. Eliot's *Old Possum's Book of Practical Cats* is said to have inspired the long-running Broadway musical *Cats*, composed by Andrew Lloyd Webber. New York City's show at the Winter Garden Theatre ran from 1982 to 2000, and in its first year won seven Tony Awards, including Best Musical. Eliot's 1982 edition of *Old Possum's* was illustrated by another documented cat lover, Edward Gorey.

- If your cat gives you a look at its back end, you could call it a back-handed compliment: a raised tail with a glimpse of its rear is a cat's way of showing it feels safe with you.

Zoom

Disrupted

Distracted

Everybody Says Meow

Working from Home with a Cat

TITLES BY: Istvan Banyai / Dan Lyons / James Lang / Constance Lombardo / Heidi Moreno

ZOOM

Disrupted   DAN

Distracted   Why Students Can't Focus

EVERYBODY SAYS MEOW

MORENO   WORKING FROM HOME
          WITH A CAT   CHRONICLE BOOKS

HAW
ELLIS
THE TRAINABLE CAT

LAUGH OUT LOUD 40 Women Hu

The Trainable Cat

Laugh Out Loud

- "Dogs like everyone. Cats choose who to like."
  —Lauren Myracle, *Shine*, 2011

- "You know how it is with cats: They don't really have owners, they have staff."
  —P. C. Cast, *Chosen*, 2008

- "My dear, I'm a cat. Everything I see is mine."
  —Rick Riordan, *The Red Pyramid*, 2010

- Cats don't laugh, but if their ears move forward, their tails point down, and they purr, they're pleased.

- The origins of "LOL" as an acronym for "laughing out loud" are uncertain. According to linguist and writer Ben Zimmer, the first recorded use was in a May 1989 newsletter of FidoNet, a computer network created by Tom Jennings to exchange email, files, and other news among users of bulletin-board systems, especially popular before the internet. However, a man named Wayne Pearson claims he coined the acronym on a bulletin-board system called Viewline in Calgary, Alberta, Canada, in the early to mid-1980s. "LOL" was added to the *Oxford English Dictionary* in 2011. Its plural, "LOLZ," made the Scrabble dictionary in 2015.

- To cachinnate is to laugh loudly and heartily. From the Latin *cachinnare*, it was likely coined in imitation of the sound. The word "cackle" comes from the Middle English *cakelen*, also, it is believed, after the sound.

TITLES BY: John Bradshaw and Sarah Ellis / Allia Zobel Nolan

- "Can you define 'plan' as 'a loose sequence of manifestly inadequate observations and conjectures, held together by panic, indecision, and ignorance'? If so, it was a very good plan."
—Jonathan Stroud, *The Ring of Solomon*, 2010

- "At that rate, I'd be lucky if I wrote a page a day."
—Sylvia Plath, *The Bell Jar*, 1963

- "Why? Do you find this . . . distracting?"
—Suzanne Collins, *Mockingjay*, 2010

- In his 2018 book, *Hyperfocus: How to Be More Productive in a World of Distraction*, Chris Bailey says our brains are predisposed to distraction, wandering for an average of 47 percent of the day. At a computer, we typically work only forty seconds before we're distracted or interrupted.

- *The Secret of the Old Clock*, the first book in the Nancy Drew mystery series by Carolyn Keene, was published in 1930, with artwork by Russell H. Tandy. Carolyn Keene was the pen name of the authors of the Nancy Drew and the Dana Girls mystery series, produced by Stratemeyer Syndicate, as well as the Nancy Drew spin-off series for preteens, River Heights, published by Simon & Schuster in 1989. Nancy Drew's writers, beginning with Mildred Wirt Benson, were hired by Edward Stratemeyer, founder of the syndicate, for $125 per book. They were required to give up all rights to the work and maintain authorship confidentiality. At least eleven ghostwriters contributed to the series, though Benson is credited as the primary Carolyn Keene. Harriet Stratemeyer Adams, Edward's daughter, took over the voice of Nancy Drew in the 1950s, rewriting eight books and writing twenty-six more.

In Memory of Memory

I Used to Have a Plan

The Way Things Work Now

I Can't Keep My Own Secrets

Concentration

Oh Look, a Cake!

TITLES BY: Maria Stepanova, translated by Sasha Dugdale / Alessandra Olanow / David Macaulay / Smith Magazine / Stefan Van der Stigchel, translated by Danny Guinan / J. C. McKee

In Memory of Memory • *Maria Stepanova* NDP1489

I USED TO HAVE A PLAN   ALESSANDRA OLANOW

THE WAY THINGS WORK
DAVID MACAULAY

SIX-WORD MEMOIRS BY TEENS FAMOUS & OBSCURE | I CAN'T KEEP MY OWN SECRETS | EDITED BY SMITH MAGAZINE | HARPER TEEN

Stefan Van der Stigchel CONCENTRATION

.McKEE OH LOOK, A CAKE! Clarion Books

The COMEDY of SURVIVAL
IN SEARCH OF AN ENVIRONMENTAL ETHIC

🕐 **Performance Reviews**

The Comedy of Survival

Performance Reviews

- "Just keep swimming."
  —Dory from *Finding Nemo*, 2003

- "A learning experience is one of those things that says, 'You know that thing you just did? Don't do that.'"
  —Douglas Adams, *The Salmon of Doubt: Hitchhiking the Galaxy One Last Time*, 2002

- "I have a business appointment that I am anxious . . . to miss."
  —Oscar Wilde, *The Importance of Being Earnest*, 1895

- "All hope abandon ye who enter here." It only *feels* like a warning for your performance review. It's the message on the gate to Hell in Dante Alighieri's epic poem *The Divine Comedy*, 1320. At first, Dante titled the work *La Commedia* (*The Comedy*) because despite its beginnings in Hell, the poem ends in Heaven's pleasures.   .

- A 2019 Gallup study found that only 14 percent of employees strongly agree their performance reviews inspire them to improve. Thirty-three percent of the time, reviews made performance worse. Robert Sutton and Ben Wigert, authors of the May 6, 2019, Gallup Workplace article, "More Harm Than Good: The Truth About Performance Reviews," wrote, "In other words, if performance reviews were a drug, they would not meet FDA approval for efficacy."

TITLES BY: Joseph W. Meeker / Harvard Business Review

- "Most people do not listen with the intent to understand; they listen with the intent to reply."
—Stephen R. Covey, *The 7 Habits of Highly Effective People*, 1989

- "One cannot think well, love well, sleep well, if one has not dined well."
—Virginia Woolf, *A Room of One's Own*, 1929

- In the 1950s sitcom *Father Knows Best*, Robert Young played Jim Anderson, a married dad of three living in the fictional town of Springfield. The series was adapted from a radio program that began in 1949, also starring Robert Young. CBS canceled the show in 1955, but fan protests led to NBC's picking it up and making it a hit.

- Matt Groening, creator of *The Simpsons*, chose Springfield for the town's name because as a kid he believed *Father Knows Best* had taken place in Springfield, Oregon, near his own hometown of Portland. Groening's dad, Homer, was named after the epic poet who wrote *The Iliad* and *The Odyssey*. Groening's grandmother, Homer's mother, named another son Victor Hugo.

- Playwright William Saroyan's first novel, *The Human Comedy*, began as a script for MGM. The novel was adapted from the screenplay, which won the 1944 Academy Award for Best Writing, Original Motion Picture Story. Its plot followed the daily life of fourteen-year-old Homer Macauley and his family—which included his younger brother, Ulysses, and his older brother, Marcus, a soldier—during World War II. Three years earlier, Saroyan had declined the Pulitzer Prize for Drama for his 1939 play *The Time of Your Life*, saying, "I do not believe in prizes or awards in the realm of art."

Like My Father Always Said . . .

Listen to Your Mother

Listen to Your Heart

Listen to Your Gut

What's for Dinner?

TITLES BY: Erin McHugh / Ann Imig / Kasie West / Jini Patel Thompson / Curtis Stone

LIKE MY FATHER ALWAYS SAID...   Erin McHugh   ABR

LISTEN TO YOUR MOTHER

LISTEN TO YOUR HEART

CARAMAL PUBLISHING

Listen
TO YOUR **GUT**

THE
Natural
FO

WHAT'S FOR DINNER? Ballantine Books

True Comfort Krist

The Dinner Herm

LATER PAUL LISICKY

ON DIAMOND THE SPRAWL

True Comfort

The Dinner

Later

The Sprawl

- "She planned to make a roast beef, a pile of mashed potatoes, corn— then mound it into a bowl and drown it in gravy. Some people ate ice cream or pie when depressed; she went for the warm comfort food she learned to make in her grandma's kitchen."
—Amy E. Reichert, *The Coincidence of Coconut Cake*, 2015

- "For the next few minutes—the first peaceful minutes she'd shared with her daughter since she'd arrived—the two of them ate, letting the sticky, wholesome goodness melt on their tongues and stick to their palates and fill their mouths with that internal hug of a cherished comfort food."
- —Sonali Dev, *Recipe for Persuasion*, 2020

- "Food is meant to feed more than an empty belly. It's also meant to nourish your heart."
- —Elizabeth Acevedo, *With the Fire on High*, 2019

- "After a good dinner one can forgive anybody, even one's own relations."
- —Oscar Wilde, *A Woman of No Importance*, Lady Caroline, act 2, 1893

- "The counsel that is given after dinner is not always the best."
—Philippe de Commines, *The Memoirs of Philippe de Commines*, 1524–1528

- A digestif is an alcoholic beverage served after a meal to aid digestion. In liqueurs, digestifs such as amaro, port, sherry, aquavit, and chartreuse often contain stomach-settling herbs like fennel, caraway, anise, and lemon verbena, and have a bittersweet taste. Though an after-dinner cup of coffee is a classic nonalcoholic digestif, its caffeine can also act as a stimulant.

- To nid-nod is to nod repeatedly when you're sleepy.

TITLES BY: Kristin Cavallari / Herman Koch / Paul Lisicky / Jason Diamond

- "Oh, I just want what we all want: a comfortable couch, a nice beverage, a weekend of no distractions and a book that will stop time, lift me out of my quotidian existence and alter my thinking forever."
  —Elizabeth Gilbert, *The New York Times*, June 14, 2012

- "'Of course I cook,' I say, looking offended. 'I'm a pizza rolls aficionado.'"
  —Mikki Daughtry and Rachael Lippincott, *All This Time*, 2020

- "You gotta know when to be lazy. Done correctly, it's an art form that benefits everyone."
  —Nicholas Sparks, *The Choice*, 2007

- Tom Iaccino coined the phrase "couch potato" in 1976 on a phone call to friend Bob Armstrong as a pun on "boob tuber." Cartoonist Armstrong asked Iaccino if he could use the phrase, drew it, and later trademarked the term. "Couch potato" entered the *Oxford English Dictionary* in 1993 and was defined as a "person who spends leisure time passively or idly sitting around, especially watching television." In June 2005, the BBC reported scheduled protests by the British Potato Council, which believed the term was harmful to the spud's image and wanted it removed from the dictionary. British potato farmers gathered outside the offices of the dictionary's publisher, Oxford University Press, as well as in London's Parliament Square. The same year, the *Oxford Dictionary of New Words* added "mouse potato" as slang for one who spends a lot of time online, "an alteration of the phrase 'couch potato.'"

- Since 2007, when Apple debuted the first iPhone, the phrases "screen time" and "binge-watching" have surpassed "couch potato" in Google searches.

- If you're binge-watching *The Godfather* series, based on the books by Mario Puzo, you may find yourself getting hungry: sixty-one scenes feature food or people eating. In all three *Godfather* films, oranges in a scene indicate imminent death (or its close call).

The Order of the Day
The Couch Potato

TITLES BY: Éric Vuillard, translated by Mark Polizzotti / Jory John and Peter Oswald

THE ORDER OF THE DAY - É

THE COUCH POTATO

a Wilder FALLING into YOU

yoon EVERYTHING, EVERYTHING

SERIOUSLY DELISH JESS MERC

Falling Into You

Everything, Everything

Seriously Delish

- "As he read, I fell in love the way you fall asleep: slowly, and then all at once."
—John Green, *The Fault in Our Stars*, 2012

- "When you meet the one who makes you smile as you've never smiled before, cry as you've never cried before. . . there is nothing to do but fall."
—Renée Ahdieh, *The Wrath and the Dawn*, 2016

- "And I am utterly in love."
—Nina LaCour, *Everything Leads to You*, 2015

- "Now I'm really satisfied, because I can't think of anything better."
—Henry James, *The Portrait of a Lady*, 1881

- If you've fallen in love, you know the feeling's hard to describe. The *Oxford English Dictionary* notes an early use of the expression was "to fall (or be brought) into love's dance: c. 1500, *Kingis Quair* (1939) 'So ferr ifallyng into lufis dance.'" James Rogers's *Dictionary of Cliches* says to fall "head over heels" was originally expressed the other way around: "As early as the fourteenth century it appeared in a poem as 'hele ouer hed.'" Adrian Room's *Brewer's Dictionary of Phrase and Fable* defines falling in love as being "sexually attracted to a person; to become very fond of a thing." He writes, "'Fall' here did not originally have the present sense of dropping from a higher state to a lower, but of passing suddenly from one state to another." And the top definition of "falling in love" on urbandictionary.com says it's when someone is "the first thing you think of when you wake up, and the last thing when you fall asleep."

- The first known use of "delish" as a shortened form of "delicious" was in 1920. Other words also first seen in print that year include "al dente," "biscotto," "butter bean," "cola," "daiquiri," "guacamole," "lingonberry," and "toothbrushing."

TITLES BY: Jasinda Wilder / Nicola Yoon / Jessica Merchant

- "I judge people two ways—on how they treat animals, and on what they like to eat. If their favorite food is some kind of salad, they are definitely a bad person. Anything with cheese, they are probably OK."
—Catriona Ward, *The Last House on Needless Street*, 2021

- "This was fresh, rich, heavenly, succulent, soft, creamy, kiss-my-ass, cows-gotta-die-for-this, delightfully salty, moo-ass, good old white folks cheese, cheese to die for, cheese to make you happy, cheese to beat the cheese boss, cheese for the big cheese, cheese to end the world. . . ."
—James McBride, *Deacon King Kong*, 2020

- "Then he brought her a large slice of bread and a piece of the golden cheese, and told her to eat."
—Johanna Spyri, *Heidi*, illustrated by Jessie Willcox Smith, 1922

- Someone who loves cheese is a turophile, from the Greek word for cheese, *tyros*, and the English "-phile," meaning lover. "-Phile" itself came from the Greek *philos*, meaning "loving." Although the word can be traced to the 1930s, it never really caught on with cheese lovers. The fear of cheese is known as turophobia.

- Martha Lloyd, a friend of novelist Jane Austen, who lived with Austen, her sister Cassandra, and their mother (also called Cassandra) in Chawton, Hampshire, shares how to make the author's favorite cheese toastie in *Martha Lloyd's Household Book: The Original Manuscript from Jane Austen's Kitchen*, published in 2021 by the Bodleian Library, University of Oxford: "Grate the cheese & add it to one egg, & a teaspoonful of Mustard, & a little Butter. Send it up on a toast or in paper Trays."

- The heart symbol became popular during the Renaissance, when it was used in religious art to depict the Sacred Heart of Christ, as well as one of the four suits on playing cards.

- I ♥ NY is the official slogan of New York State. Renowned graphic designer Milton Glaser sketched the iconic logo with a red crayon on the back of an envelope during a taxi ride, for a 1977 campaign to promote tourism in the state.

I Want You to Know

What I Know for Sure

Three Little Words

I Heart Cheese

TITLES BY: Leslie Cottrell Simonds / Oprah Winfrey / Ashley Rhodes-Courter / Mihaela Metaxa-Albu

i want you to know

rey   What I Know For Sure  FLAT IRON BOOKS

HLEY
COURTER   three little words   A Memoir

I ♥ CHEESE: A C

THE SADDEST WORDS

WILLIAM FAULKNER'S CIVIL WAR

THE BIGGEST
BLUFF

KO

STEPHEN WRIGHT

PROCESSED CHEESE

The Saddest Words

The Biggest Bluff

Processed Cheese

- "This is the saddest story I have ever heard."
—Ford Madox Ford, *The Good Soldier*, 1915

- In 2013, readers of *Rolling Stone* magazine chose Eric Clapton's "Tears in Heaven" as the number one saddest song of all time. Written in 1991 by Clapton and Will Jennings as a tribute to Clapton's son, who fell to his death at the age of four, the song swept the Grammys. By 2004, Clapton chose not to sing it, and dropped the song from his shows for nine years.

- "Science is a way to call the bluff of those who only pretend to knowledge."
—Carl Sagan, *The Demon-Haunted World: Science as a Candle in the Dark*, 1995

- "If you're that clever you can argue yourself into anything."
—Julian Barnes, *The Sense of an Ending*, 2011

- "When my brain begins to reel from my literary labors, I make an occasional cheese dip."
—John Kennedy Toole, *A Confederacy of Dunces*, 1980

- Whether in a loaf, a sauce, a spread, or a spray, processed cheese typically contains about 50 percent real cheese.

TITLES BY: Michael Gorra / Maria Konnikova / Stephen Wright

- "Housekeeping ain't no joke."
  —Louisa May Alcott, *Little Women*, 1868

- In a November 2010 interview with Oprah Winfrey to promote his memoir, George W. Bush recalled, "So, I'm lying on the couch and Laura walks in and I say, 'Free at last,' and she says, 'You're free, all right, you're free to do the dishes.' So I say, 'You're talking to the former president, baby,' and she said, 'Consider this your new domestic policy agenda.'"

- A 2016 study published in the *Journal of Marriage and Family* found when heterosexual couples share chores, they have more sex. In April 2018, Wisconsin Public Radio reported findings by the American Sociological Association that, especially for women in couples of different genders, "it's sharing who does the dishes—more than any other household chore—that coincides with a couple's well-being." In July 2021, *The Irish Times* reported research by the Central Statistics Offices that compared opposite-sex to same-sex couples. The same-sex couples described a more balanced sharing of tasks, fewer disagreements, and higher levels of satisfaction.

- In 1883, Josephine Cochran, a Chicago socialite, tired of her heirloom dishes becoming chipped from the hired help's washing and not enamored of the chore herself, designed the first dishwashing machine to use water pressure. Her invention, patented in 1886, is considered the first commercially viable dishwasher. She made the machines in a shed behind her house and began advertising in local papers as the Garis-Cochran Dish Washing Machine Company. Hotels and restaurants, like Chicago's Palmer House and the Sherman House Hotel, soon supported her. When Cochran unveiled the dishwasher at the World's Columbian Exhibition of 1893—the only invention presented by a woman—she received great interest. She renamed her business the Crescent Washing Machine Company around 1898, when she opened her own factory. Though Cochran died in 1913, in 1917 she received a posthumous patent for an improved dishwasher. In 1926, her company was acquired by Hobart under the KitchenAid brand, which was acquired by Whirlpool in 1986. Cochran was inducted into the National Inventors Hall of Fame in 2006.

Taking Turns

Cleaning Up

This Is the Story of a Happy Marriage

TITLES BY: MK Czerwiec / Barry Minkow / Ann Patchett

Czerwiec **Taking Turns** Stories from HIV

CLEANING UP BA

ETT *This Is the Story of a Happy Marriage*

A BURNING   MEGHA MAJUMDAR

A Strange Stirring   BASIC BOOKS

cooking for one

AND I DO NOT FORGIVE YOU

A Burning

A Strange Stirring

Cooking for One

And I Do Not Forgive You

TITLES BY: Megha Majumdar / Stephanie Coontz / America's Test Kitchen / Amber Sparks

- "When he is late for dinner and I know he must either be having / an affair or lying dead in the middle of the street, / I always hope he's dead."
  —Judith Viorst, *It's Hard to Be Hip over Thirty (And Other Tragedies of Married Life)*, 1968

- "Burning dinner is not incompetence but war."
  —Marge Piercy, "What's That Smell in the Kitchen?" *Stone, Paper, Knife*, 1983

- "It is a fire which consumes me, but I am the fire."
  —Jorge Luis Borges, *Labyrinths: Selected Stories & Other Writings*, 1962

- "This time I wouldn't forget him, because I couldn't ever forgive him—*for breaking my heart twice*."
  —James Patterson and Gabrielle Charbonnet, *Sundays at Tiffany's*, 2008

- According to Jess McHugh's *Americanon: An Unexpected U.S. History in Thirteen Bestselling Books*, Betty Crocker's Picture Cook Book has sold more than 75 million copies since its 1950 publication, making it the bestselling cookbook in American history. "Betty" was born in 1921, when flour-maker the Washburn-Crosby Company decided they needed a persona to respond to the overwhelming number of baking questions they received after a promotion they'd held for their Gold Medal Flour. They came up with the name Betty, and chose her surname to honor retired company director William G. Crocker. The fictional Betty Crocker became so famous that in 1945 *Fortune* magazine named her the second best-known woman in America, behind Eleanor Roosevelt.

- The word "stir-fry" was first used in the 1945 cookbook, *How to Cook and Eat in Chinese* by Buwei Yang Chao. The word was created by Yang's husband, Yuen Ren Chao, a linguist who loved translating and playing with words and their meanings. The couple is also credited with coining the English word for Chinese dumplings, "pot stickers."

- "She ate—so, so good—cocooned in the harmonic dissonance of a large family, where every sound was distinct yet blended."
  —Rachel Hauck, *The Writing Desk*, 2017

- "May the memory of this moment, here, the glowing impression of the two of us facing each other in this warm, bright place, drinking lovely hot tea, help save him, even a little bit."
  —Banana Yoshimoto, *Kitchen*, 1988

- "And now I have to stop. Because every time I remember this, I have to cry a little by myself. I don't know why something that made me so happy then feels so sad now. Maybe that is the way it is with the best memories."
  —Amy Tan, *The Kitchen God's Wife*, 1991

- Spoons have been around since prehistoric times, as natural materials were adapted as eating utensils. The Greek and Latin words for "spoon" come from *cochlea*, meaning a spiral shell; the Anglo-Saxon word *spon* means a chip of wood. By the Middle Ages, royalty and other wealthy people used spoons made of precious metals. When pewter became common in the fourteenth century, spoons became affordable to the general population.

- The Duke of Hastings—or rather, his spoon—has an Instagram account. In episode three of the Netflix series *Bridgerton*, the duke, played by Regé-Jean Page, is at a tea shop with love interest Daphne, where he licks cream off the spoon. The episode aired on December 25, 2020; Billie Bhatia created the account—@thedukesspoon—shortly after. By May 2021, the account had nearly twenty-four thousand followers.

- *Bridgerton*, produced by Shonda Rhimes, was adapted from a series of romance novels about London in the 1800s by author Julia Quinn. The first book, *The Duke and I*, was published in 2000. After the show aired, it reached number one on *The New York Times* best-seller list, with two other *Bridgerton* books ranking in the top ten.

Sanctuary

Our Little Kitchen
A Place at the Table
Licking the Spoon

TITLES BY: Paola Mendoza and Abby Sher / Jillian Tamaki / Saadia Faruqi and Laura Shovan / Candace Walsh

ZA **SANCTUARY** putnam

ki Our Little Kitchen ABRAM

Shovan A Place at the Table Clarion Books

Licking the Spoon A MEMOIR OF FOOD, FAMILY AND

ridiculous / hilarious / terrible / cool

OTHER WORDS for Home

.ooper

Ridiculous / Hilarious / Terrible / Cool
Other Words for Home

- "Perhaps home is not a place but simply an irrevocable condition."
  —James Baldwin, *Giovanni's Room*, 1956

- "I used to dream about escaping my ordinary life, but my life was never ordinary. I had simply failed to notice how extraordinary it was. Likewise, I never imagined that home might be something I would miss."
  —Ransom Riggs, *Miss Peregrine's Home for Peculiar Children*, 2011

- Home. Sweet or otherwise, there's no place like it. The origin of the famous phrase is often attributed to the 1823 song "Home, Sweet Home," with words by John Payne and music by Sir Henry Bishop. The song includes the line "There's no place like home." In his later life, Bishop claimed to have also written the lyrics. However, neither Bishop nor Payne coined the phrase. The proverb had been used and documented in England long before the song came to be.

- "There's no place like home" entered the pop culture pantheon when it was delivered by Dorothy Gale, played by Judy Garland, in the 1939 musical film *The Wizard of Oz*, which was based on L. Frank Baum's 1900 children's fantasy and directed mainly by Victor Fleming. Fleming left production to take over the direction of *Gone with the Wind*, based on the novel by Margaret Mitchell. *Oz* garnered six Academy Award nominations, including Best Picture, which it lost—to Fleming's *Gone with the Wind*.

- In L. Frank Baum's book, Dorothy's ruby shoes are silver.

- In a 1903 press release he wrote to announce the reissue of *The Wonderful Wizard of Oz*, Baum said he came up with the name Oz while looking at his filing cabinet. "The first was A–G; the next drawer was labeled H–N; and on the last were the letters, O–Z. And 'Oz' it at once became."

TITLES BY: Elisha Cooper / Jasmine Warga

- "All happy families are alike; each unhappy family is unhappy in its own way."
  —Leo Tolstoy, *Anna Karenina*, 1877

- "And hopefully I have changed, you know, as a person. But honestly, if I have, it's because of you."
  —Sally Rooney, *Normal People*, 2018

- "You must remember, family is often born of blood, but it doesn't *depend* on blood. Nor is it exclusive of friendship. Family members can be your best friends, you know. And best friends, whether or not they are related to you, can be your family."
  —Trenton Lee Stewart, *The Mysterious Benedict Society*, 2007

- On her website, Appalachian poet George Ella Lyon says she wrote *Where I'm From* in 1993 in response to a poem from *Stories I Ain't Told Nobody Yet* by her friend, Tennessee poet Jo Carson. As Kentucky's poet laureate in 2015, Lyon, along with the Kentucky Arts Council collected 731 *Where I'm From* poems from eighty-three countries around the world. In 2019, NPR resident poet Kwame Alexander and host Rachel Martin asked listeners for their memories of home. In two days, they received fourteen hundred submissions.

- Gerald Durrell's *My Family and Other Animals*, the first book in the Corfu Trilogy (its sequels are *Birds, Beasts and Relatives* and *The Garden of the Gods*), is the British naturalist's account of his childhood on the Greek island, sharing a villa with bats, butterflies, scorpions, pigeons, octopuses, and gulls. His memories of home inspired the PBS Masterpiece production of *The Durrells in Corfu*.

Where Do I Begin?
It's Kind of a Funny Story
Where I'm From

I Am Who I Am Because . . .
My Family and Other Animals

But Seriously

TITLES BY: Elvis Duran / Ned Vizzini / George Ella Lyon / Willie (Mac) McDaniel / Gerald Durrell / John McEnroe

DURAN _Where Do I Begin?_ ATRIA BOOKS

VIZZINI  IT'S KIND OF A FUNNY STORY HYPERION

Lyon _where i'm from_ ABSEY & CO.

I AM WHO I AM BECAUSE...

RALD RRELL MY FAMILY AND OTHER ANIMALS

ENROE **BUT SERIOUSLY** BACK BAY BOOKS

I Have Something to Tell You　CH

bbri

I Am a Capybara

t. REYNOLDS　　　SAY SOMETHING!　　　ORCHARD

I Have Something to Tell You

I Am a Capybara

Say Something!

- "I believe there is power in words, power in asserting our existence, our experience, our lives, through words."
  —Jesmyn Ward, from the introduction to *The Fire This Time: A New Generation Speaks About Race*, 2016

- "People are too complicated to have simple labels."
  —Philip Pullman, *The Amber Spyglass*, 2000

- "When I was born, the name for what I was did not exist."
  —Madeline Miller, *Circe*, 2018

- "I'm not flaunting anything. I'm just existing. This is me."
  —Kacen Callender, *Felix Ever After*, 2020

- "He allowed himself to be swayed by his conviction that human beings are not born once and for all on the day their mothers give birth to them, but that life obliges them over and over again to give birth to themselves."
  —Gabriel García Márquez, *Love in the Time of Cholera*, 1988

- "A rose by any other name would smell as sweet."
  —William Shakespeare, *Romeo and Juliet*, act 2, scene 2, 1597

- Indigenous to South America, the capybara is the biggest rodent on Earth. As an adult, the animal may be as long as three feet, as tall as two, and weigh up to 132 pounds. Like beavers, these semiaquatic mammals, similar in shape to a pig, are strong swimmers. They typically live in groups of ten to twenty, and they love to eat plants.

TITLES BY: Chasten Buttigieg / Michela Fabbri / Peter H. Reynolds

- "We're all a little weird. And life is a little weird. And when we find someone whose weirdness is compatible with ours, we join up with them and fall into mutually satisfying weirdness—and call it love—true love."
  —Robert Fulghum, *True Love*, 1997

- "Nobody wants to be here and nobody wants to leave."
  —Cormac McCarthy, *The Road*, 2006

- According to Keith Houston's book *Shady Characters: The Secret Life of Punctuation, Symbols & Other Typographical Marks*, the first ampersand appeared in graffiti in the volcanic ash of Pompeii. The symbol was a ligature, a character made of two or more letters joined together. In this case, an *e* and a *t*, a form of the Latin word *et*, meaning "and." In English, in the late Middle Ages, *per se* was often added to letters that could stand alone as words. The ampersand symbol was called "& per se, and," which eventually evolved into the word "ampersand."

- "Whatever"? Or "what ever"? Traditionally, the one-word "whatever" was a pronoun, as in "*Whatever* you do, don't do that," while the two-word "what ever" was used for emphasis: "What *ever* do you mean?" Today, "whatever" is most used as an interjection, often dismissively: "Yeah, whatever." The *Oxford English Dictionary* labels the usage colloquial and says it originated in the United States, citing an example from a 1965 episode of the TV series *Bewitched*, as Samantha's mother, Endora, consistently mispronounces her son-in-law's name:

Endora: "Good morning, Derwood."

Samantha: "Darrin."

Endora: "Whatever."

Between You & Me

I'm Fine and Neither Are You

Whatever . . . Love Is Love

Lucky Us

TITLES BY: Mary Norris / Camille Pagán / Maria Bello / Amy Bloom

BETWEEN YOU & ME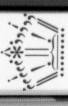

I'M FINE AND NEITHER ARE YOU

BELLO | whatever... LOVE IS LOVE DEY ST.

 LUCKY US A

BRYSON A Walk in the Woods BIDWY

DAD BY MY SIDE

ABOVE US THE MILKY WAY   AN ILLUM NATED A BA

TENDER IS THE NIGHT   F. SCOT

A Walk in the Woods

Dad by My Side

Above Us the Milky Way

Tender Is the Night

- "Moonless, this June night is all the more alive with stars."
  —Aldous Huxley, *Music at Night and Other Essays*, 1931

- "I believe that what we become depends on what our fathers teach us at odd moments, when they aren't trying to teach us."
  —Umberto Eco, *Foucault's Pendulum*, 1988

- "To what end, he wondered, had the Divine created the stars in heaven to fill a man with feelings of inspiration one day and insignificance the next?"
  —Amor Towles, *A Gentleman in Moscow*, 2016

- The Milky Way candy bar was created in 1920 and trademarked in 1925 by Frank Clarence Mars, founder of the MAR-O-BAR candy company. Mars is said to have invented the candy in his kitchen at home with the windows wide open. Consequently, one of the first print ads listed as ingredients "sunlight and fresh air." In 1926, the bar was available in two flavors, chocolate and vanilla, and sold for a nickel. In 1936, the vanilla bar, which was covered in dark chocolate, was renamed the Forever Yours bar. It was discontinued in 1979. In 1989 it returned as Milky Way Dark, then was renamed again in 2000 as Milky Way Midnight.

- F. Scott Fitzgerald's fourth and final novel, *Tender Is the Night*, takes its title from the poem "Ode to a Nightingale" by John Keats. First serialized in four issues of *Scribner's Magazine*, the novel was published by Charles Scribner's Sons in April 1934. *Tender Is the Night* was not an immediate success. In its first three months, only twelve thousand copies sold; comparatively, Fitzgerald's *This Side of Paradise* sold more than fifty thousand copies during the same period.

TITLES BY: Bill Bryson / Soosh / Fowzia Karimi / F. Scott Fitzgerald

- " 'WELCOME TO EXPECTATIONS,' " said a carefully lettered sign on a small house at the side of the road. " 'INFORMATION, PREDICTIONS, AND ADVICE CHEERFULLY OFFERED. PARK HERE AND BLOW HORN.' "
  —Norton Juster, *The Phantom Tollbooth*, illustrated by Jules Feiffer, 1961

- "This was the trouble with families. Like invidious doctors, they knew just where it hurt."
  —Arundhati Roy, *The God of Small Things*, 1997

- According to *The Undead Eighteenth Century* by Linda Troost, zombies appeared in literature as far back as 1697, though more as spirits or ghosts than brain-eating monsters.

- *World War Z*, written by Max Brooks in 2006, inspired the 2013 film of the same name. Produced by and starring Brad Pitt, it is the highest-grossing zombie film to date. On his website, Brooks, who has posted a quote that cites him as "the Studs Terkel of zombie journalism," says his work inspired the U.S. military to examine responses to possible future crises. A fellow at the Modern War Institute at West Point, Brooks has coedited two books on teaching military science through science fiction: *Strategy Strikes Back: How "Star Wars" Explains Modern Military Conflict* and *Winning Westeros: How "Game of Thrones" Explains Modern Military Conflict*.

- Not that family has *anything* to do with conflict: the Guinness World Record for the largest family reunion was set on August 12, 2012, when direct descendants of seventeenth-century couple Georges Porteau and Madeleine Boileve got together for the day in Saint-Paul-Mont-Pénit, Vendée, France. All 4,514 of them.

- The word "pandemonium" was coined by John Milton in his epic poem, "Paradise Lost" (1667), from the Greek prefix *pan-*, meaning "all," and the Latin word *daemonium*, meaning "evil spirit." Pandæmonium was the name of the palace in the middle of Hell, where all the demons lived.

Zombie Family Reunion

Things Fall Apart

TITLES BY: Zack Zombie / Chinua Achebe

ZOMBIE FAMILY REUNION

THINGS FALL APART

Out the **Door**

MUDBOUND

'Turk   MUDDY   The Story of Blu

Derby   Outside in

Out the Door

Mudbound

Muddy

Outside In

- "Mud is to jump in and slide in and yell doodleedoodleedo."
—Ruth Krauss, *A Hole Is to Dig*, 1952

- "When she trod on mud, the mud was beautiful; when she ran in the rain, the rain was silver."
—C. S. Lewis, *Till We Have Faces*, 1956

- "It's kind of peaceful lying here among the dandelions."
—Charles M. Schulz, *Peanuts*, April 3, 1965

- Hillary Jordan's 2006 *Mudbound* won the Bellwether Award, established by author Barbara Kingsolver, the nation's largest prize for an unpublished manuscript of a novel. In 2012, the award for writings on social justice became known as the PEN/Bellwether Prize for Socially Engaged Fiction.

- *Mudbound* was adapted into a 2017 Netflix film directed by Dee Rees. The film earned four Academy Award nominations, including Best Cinematography, making Rachel Morrison the first woman to be nominated in that category. Rees was the first Black woman nominated for Best Adapted Screenplay.

- *Outside In*, written by Deborah Underwood and illustrated by Cindy Derby, won Derby a 2021 Caldecott Honor from the American Library Association. The Caldecott Medal that year went to Tlingit artist Michaela Goade for her illustrations in Carole Lindstrom's *We Are Water Protectors*. Goade became the first BIPOC woman and the first Indigenous person to win the medal. Marcia Brown (1918–2015) is the most recognized Caldecott artist, with three medals and six honor books. Only author/illustrator David Wiesner has also won three.

TITLES BY: Christy Hale / Hillary Jordan / Michael Mahin and Evan Turk / Deborah Underwood and Cindy Derby

- "Look at everything always as though you were seeing it either for the first or last time: Thus is your time on earth filled with glory."
  —Betty Smith, *A Tree Grows in Brooklyn*, 1943

- "If I had influence with the good fairy who is supposed to preside over the christening of all children I should ask that her gift to each child in the world be a sense of wonder so indestructible that it would last throughout life."
  —Rachel Carson, *The Sense of Wonder*, 1956

- "I shouldn't wonder if you didn't wonder much too much!"
  —P. L. Travers, *Mary Poppins Comes Back*, 1935

- *The Promised Land*, by Barack Obama, broke all sales records for publisher Penguin Random House in 2020. The former president's memoir sold 887,000 copies its first day on sale, more than 1.7 million copies its first week, and more than 3 million a month after publication.

Dirt

A Promised Land

Where Wonder Grows

TITLES BY: Bill Buford / Barack Obama / Xelena González and Adriana M. Garcia

DIRT BILL BU

A | A PROMISED LAND

CROWN

WHERE WONDER GROWS XELENA

Fleischman   SEEDFOLKS

 ⵣⵍⵓⵓⵜⵣⵙ

ra   JUMP at the SUN

 Bloom

Seedfolks

Uprooted

Jump at the Sun

Bloom

- "The fairest thing in nature, a flower, still has its roots in earth and manure."
  —D. H. Lawrence, from the introduction to *Pansies*, 1929

- "There is room enough for a world between a lilac and a wall."
  —Michael Pollan, *Second Nature: A Gardener's Education*, 1991

- "Did u hear about the rose that grew from a crack in the concrete"
  —Tupac Shakur, *The Rose That Grew from Concrete*, 1999

- Angie Thomas, author of 2021's *Concrete Rose*, says her book about a seventeen-year-old single dad (who grows up to become the father of Starr in *The Hate U Give*) was inspired by Tupac Shakur and his poetry. The title, like Shakur's, nods to the flower that thrives despite its environment.

- The picture book *Jump at the Sun: The True Life Tale of Unstoppable Storycatcher Zora Neale Hurston* by Newbery Honor winner Alicia D. Williams and illustrator Jacqueline Alcántara, follows the legendary writer from her childhood in Florida through her success in New York. The book's title is an expression Zora's mother used to tell her daughter to reach beyond her goals.

TITLES BY: Paul Fleischman / Naomi Novik / Alicia D. Williams and Jacqueline Alcántara / Kevin Panetta and Savanna Ganucheau

- "It was green, the silence; the light was moist; / the month of June trembled like a butterfly."
  —Pablo Neruda, "Sonnet XL," from *100 Love Sonnets*, 1959, translated by Stephen Tapscott, 1986

- "In June, / the tomato / cuts loose, / invades / the kitchens, / takes over lunches, / sits down / comfortably / on sideboards, / among the glasses, / the butter dishes, / the blue salt shakers."
  —Pablo Neruda, "Ode to the Tomato," from *Full Woman, Fleshy Apple, Hot Moon: Selected Poems of Pablo Neruda*, translated by Stephen Mitchell, 1997

- "On a good day, with the sun shining and the soil warmer than the air, knowing that the best BLT in the world is a couple of weeks or months away, it seems like every dollar, every fight with a contractor and a deer was worth it."
  —William Alexander, on his book *The $64 Tomato* (2006), NPR interview, May 2006

- "If it could only be like this always—always summer, always alone, the fruit always ripe . . ."
  —Evelyn Waugh, *Brideshead Revisited*, 1945

- The tomato is thought to have originated in Peru. The name in English comes from the Aztec *xitomatl*, which means "plump thing with a navel." The tomatoes introduced to Europe by the Spanish in the 1500s were likely yellow; Italians called them *pomi d'oro*, or "apples of gold." When Moors in Spain brought the tomato back to Morocco, they called them *pomi dei mori*, or "apples of the Moors." Perhaps due to misheard interpretations, the French called tomatoes *pommes d'amour*, which translates in English to "apples of love." Early English cookbooks suggested cooking tomatoes for hours. C. Claiborne Ray, in *The New York Times* Q&A on July 5, 1994, concluded the cooks at the time were "suspicious that what the French called a love apple . . . was a dangerously powerful aphrodisiac."

Green

Green on Green

When Green Becomes Tomatoes

The Most Beautiful Thing

Thank You, Garden

TITLES BY: Laura Vaccaro Seeger / Dianne White and Felicita Sala / Julie Fogliano and Julie Morstad / Kao Kalia Yang and Khoa Le / Liz Garton Scanlon and Simone Shin

green

GREEN ON GREEN

When Green Becomes Tomatoes

❀ The Most Beautiful Thing ❀

Shin • **Thank You, Garden**

The *Happy Ever After* Playlist

USA TODAY BESTSELLING AUTHOR
ABBY JIMENEZ

It all began with a
NOTE

When You Were Born

WIS

The Happy Ever After Playlist

It All Began with a Note

When You Were Born

- "I hope the people who wrote those songs are happy. I hope they feel it's enough. I really do because they've made me happy. And I'm only one person."
  —Stephen Chbosky, *The Perks of Being a Wallflower*, 1999

- "The whole world had changed. Only the fairy tales remained the same."
  —Lois Lowry, *Number the Stars*, 1989

- "I think we ought to live happily ever after."
  —Diana Wynne Jones, *Howl's Moving Castle*, 1986

- The owner of Omaha radio station KOWH is credited with creating in the 1950s what could be called the first playlist—the Top 40 radio format. Robert Todd Storz is said to have been at a nearby diner when he noticed that each time the waitresses were tipped, they dropped their coins in the jukebox to play the same popular songs over and over. Back at the station, rather than playing the usual block programs of recorded music and entertainment, Storz implemented a new format for listeners: the same popular songs, played over and over.

- The song "Happy Birthday" began as "Good Morning to All," a tune sisters and teachers Patty Smith Hill and Mildred J. Hill wrote in 1893. The Hills copyrighted the song's melody and sold it to music publisher the Clayton F. Summy Company, which then published it under its copyright in *Song Stories for the Kindergarten*. Somewhere along the line, "Good Morning to All" morphed into "Happy Birthday," and by 1988 Warner Chappell held the rights to the song. Those who recorded the song in music and on videos for commercial purposes were charged licensing fees until 2016, when a legal dispute between film documentarian Jennifer Nelson and Warner Chappell over the song's usage resulted in Judge George H. King's ruling: the copyright covered only specific piano arrangements of the melody, not its lyrics. Consequently, Warner Chappell had to pay back $14 million to those who had paid to use it. According to *The Guinness Book of World Records*, "Happy Birthday" is the most popular song in the English language.

TITLES BY: Abby Jimenez / H. M. Shander / Dianna Hutts Aston and E. B. Lewis

- "In the days when everything in life was fresh—because we were sixteen, seventeen—I used to blow tenor sax. Very poorly."
  —Josef Škvorecký, *The Bass Saxophone*, 1967

- Tenor saxophonist Coleman Hawkins is considered the father of the jazz saxophone. Hawkins (1904–1969), also known as "Hawk" or "Bean," played with Louis Armstrong, Sonny Rollins, Duke Ellington, Dizzy Gillespie, Thelonious Monk, and Charlie Parker, among others. Hawkins was featured as part of the 2000 series *Jazz: A Film by Ken Burns*, distributed by PBS. The promotional copy read "Coleman Hawkins startled the world with a glimpse of what jazz would become."

- Janet Tennant's biography, *Sax Appeal: Ivy Benson and Her All-Girl Band*, tells of the less well-known British musician. After playing with a series of male bandleaders in prewar London, Benson formed her own jazz group. When World War II broke out, they played throughout the country, touring army bases and providing morale-boosting shows.

- The first American ad recognized for using sex appeal to sell a product was for Woodbury's Facial Soap in 1911. From agency J. Walter Thompson, the ad's headline—"A skin you love to touch"—portrayed not just the product but the woman who used it in a sensual way. According to the Advertising Hall of Fame, the ad's creator, Helen Lansdowne Resor, "was described by the *New York Herald Tribune* as the greatest copywriter of her generation." Lansdowne Resor championed women's rights and hired and mentored women in the workplace.

- Emojipedia.org notes that the yellow Winking Face emoji, 😉, the 2015 successor to the ;) emoticon, may be used to signal a joke, flirtation, hidden meaning, or general positivity, though it is "not to be confused with the more mischievous or sexual 😏 Smirking Face." In 2013, the *Oxford English Dictionary* added the word "emoji," from the Japanese words for *e* ("picture") and *moji* ("character") and, in 2015, chose as its Word of the Year another emoji 😂, officially called the Face with Tears of Joy.

Sax Appeal

Play It Loud

Wink

TITLES BY: Janet Tennant / Brad Tolinski and Alan di Perna / Rob Harrell

NT ♯♯ SAX APPEAL

PLAY IT LOUD  ANCHOR BOOKS

RRELL WINK

The Music of What Happens

Ask Again, Yes

Silence

Not Light, but Fire

TITLES BY: Bill Konigsberg / Mary Beth Keane

TITLES BY: Shūsaku Endō, translated by William Johnston / Matthew R. Kay

MUSIC

What You Have Heard Is True

Hallelujah Anyway

The Lost Love Song

If I Never Met You

TITLES BY: Carolyn Forché / Anne Lamott

TITLES BY: Minnie Darke / Mhairi McFarlane

- "Silence is so freaking loud."
  —Sarah Dessen, *Just Listen*, 2006

- "I think about songs that it's not just what the words say, but what the melody says, and what the sound says."
  —Paul Simon, in an interview with NPR's Terry Gross, December 11, 2000

- William Faulkner was born in 1897 and spent most of his life in Oxford, Mississippi. After dropping out of the University of Mississippi a second time, twenty-four-year-old Faulkner got a job as the postmaster there. Though he kept the job for three years, he was notoriously terrible at it and was fired in 1924 after a review by a post office inspector from Corinth, Mississippi, said, among other things, "You are neglectful of your duties, in that you are a habitual reader of books and magazines, and seem reluctant to cease reading long enough to wait on the patrons." In 1929, at age thirty-two, Faulkner published *The Sound and the Fury*. He received the Nobel Prize in 1950 and France's Legion of Honor in 1951. In 1998, the Modern Library ranked the novel number six on its list of the one hundred best English-language novels of the twentieth century. In 1987, the U.S. Postal Service issued a twenty-two cent stamp with his likeness.

- Most screams heard on television and in the movies are created by doubles and voice actors. One stock scream is so well used it has a name, the Wilhelm. Originally created for the 1951 film *Distant Drums*, the scream was used in 1977 by *Star Wars* film sound designer Ben Burtt, who named it after character Private Wilhelm from the 1953 movie *The Charge at Feather River*. To date, the Wilhelm has been heard in more than four hundred films and shows, including the book-related movies *The Lost World: Jurassic Park* (1997), *Planet of the Apes* (2001), *The Hobbit: An Unexpected Journey* (2012), *The Twilight Saga: Breaking Dawn: Part 2* (2012), *Guardians of the Galaxy Vol. 2* (2017), and *Jumanji: The Next Level* (2019).

The Silence Between Us

The Sound and the Fury

Words Without Music

Well Played

TITLES BY: Alison Gervais / William Faulkner / Philip Glass / Jen DeLuca

The Silence Between Us  GE

THE SOUND AND THE FURY FAU

Words Without Music A MEMOIR P

WELL PLAYED D

ALL TOGETHER NOW

IN A SONG FOR THE DARK TIMES

 LITTLE, BROWN

SIRI, WHO AM I?

All Together Now

A Song for the Dark Times

Siri, Who Am I?

- "It was the best of times, it was the worst of times."
—Charles Dickens, *A Tale of Two Cities*, 1859

- "There are times, however, and this is one of them, when even being right feels wrong."
—Hunter S. Thompson, *Generation of Swine: Tales of Shame and Degradation in the '80's*, 1988

- "I am Sam. Sam I am."
—Dr. Seuss, *Green Eggs and Ham*, 1960

- According to Brian Jay Jones's *Becoming Dr. Seuss: Theodor Geisel and the Making of an American Imagination*, after Geisel had written *The Cat in the Hat*—using only 236 words—his publisher, Bennett Cerf, bet the author fifty dollars he couldn't write a book using just fifty words or less. Geisel's fifty-word response with a four-word title? *Green Eggs and Ham*.

- Hope Larson, author and illustrator of the book *All Together Now*, also adapted and illustrated Madeleine L'Engle's *A Wrinkle in Time* as a graphic novel. The book spent forty-four weeks on *The New York Times* Bestsellers List and won Larson an Eisner Award.

- According to a 2012 Network World report of a Chicago start-up event, keynote speaker and one of three cofounders of Siri, Dag Kittlaus, said he came up with the name for the virtual voice. He had once considered Siri as a name for his child and liked its Norwegian meaning: "beautiful woman who leads you to victory." In April 2010, Apple acquired Siri for $200 million and featured it on the iPhone 4S. Kittlaus said Steve Jobs didn't care for the name initially, but they found no alternative. Siri stayed.

TITLES BY: Hope Larson / Ian Rankin / Sam Tschida

- "I would keep her, and raise her, and love her, even if she had to teach me how to do it."
—Vanessa Diffenbaugh, *The Language of Flowers*, 2011

- "You weren't always born to the right parents. And parents didn't necessarily get the kids they were meant to raise."
—Judy Blume, *Summer Sisters*, 1998

- "No matter how close we are to another person, few human relationships are as free from strife, disagreement, and frustration as is the relationship you have with a good dog."
—Dean Koontz, *A Big Little Life: A Memoir of a Joyful Dog Named Trixie*, 2009

- A 2020 survey commissioned by Spin Master and conducted by OnePoll found the average American child will beg their parents for a pet 1,584 times before turning eighteen. Seventy-eight percent will ask for a dog. Two-thirds of parents will give in after an average three years of pleas. When they looked back at their own childhoods, 46 percent of parents said they received a pet as a present; 89 percent said it was the best gift they ever got.

- Let's respect the mischief-makers. Maurice Sendak's picture book *Where the Wild Things Are* not only won the 1964 Caldecott Medal, it inspired a "fantasy opera" composed by Oliver Knussen in 1984 and a movie by Spike Jonze and Dave Eggers in 2009. Publisher HarperCollins's website says the book is number four on the New York Public Library's list of Top Checkouts of All Time, a National Education Association's Teacher's Top 100 Books for Children, and the top picture book in *School Library Journal*'s readers survey.

Say What You Will

Children Make Terrible Pets

TITLES BY: Cammie McGovern / Peter Brown

say what you WILL

Children Make Terrible Pets

YOU ARE HERE An Owne
Dange

 HOME AT LAST

 OUR STORY BEGINS

You Are Here

Home at Last

Our Story Begins

In a January 22, 1989, essay for *The New York Times*, Ursula K. Le Guin wrote: "First sentences are doors to worlds." Let's look at a few stories' beginnings.

- "I write this sitting in the kitchen sink."
  —Dodie Smith, *I Capture the Castle*, 1948

- "First of all, let me get something straight: This is a JOURNAL, not a diary."
  —Jeff Kinney, *Diary of a Wimpy Kid*, 2007

- "This story was going to begin like all the best stories. With a school bus falling from the sky."
  —Jason Reynolds, *Look Both Ways*, 2019

- "It was a bright cold day in April, and the clocks were striking thirteen."
  —George Orwell, *1984*, 1961

- "When I think of my wife, I always think of her head."
  —Gillian Flynn, *Gone Girl*, 2005

- "All this happened, more or less."
  —Kurt Vonnegut, *Slaughterhouse-Five*, 1969

TITLES BY: Jenny Lawson / Vera B. Williams and Chris Raschka / Elissa Brent Weissman

- "It was love at first sight."
  —Joseph Heller, *Catch-22*, 1961

- "Now she looks pale and small, but her eyes make me think of wide-open skies that I have never actually seen, only dreamed of."
  —Veronica Roth, *Allegiant*, 2013

- "She was bendable light; she shone around every corner of my day."
  —Jerry Spinelli, *Stargirl*, 2000

- A beam of light takes about 8.3 minutes to travel from the sun to Earth.

- Moonlight is reflected sunlight. After the sun's light travels to the moon, it reflects back to Earth in about 1.3 seconds.

- Shaun Tan's wordless graphic novel *The Arrival* shows one immigrant's experience in a new land. Among its many honors, the 2007 book received a *Boston Globe*-Horn Book Award Special Citation, won the Australian Book Industry Book of the Year Award, and was chosen as *The New York Times* Best Illustrated Children's Book of the Year. In 2011, Tan won his first Oscar for Best Short Animated Film for *The Lost Thing*.

The Arrival

A Velocity of Being

Every Color of Light

Squint

Hello Baby!

Raybearer

TITLES BY: Shaun Tan / Maria Popova and Claudia Bedrick / Hiroshi Osada and Ryōji Arai, translated by David Boyd / Chad Morris and Shelly Brown / Mem Fox and Steve Jenkins / Jordan Ifueko

TAN   THE ARRIVAL 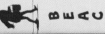 ARTHUR A. L

A Velocity of Being

Every Color of Light   ENCHAN

 SQUINT   MORRIS/BROWN

enkins   **Hello Baby!**    BEACH Ja

 KO: RAYBEARER   AMULET

WHILE YOU WERE NAPPING
THE BEAR ATE YOUR SANDWICH

IT WASN'T ME

nieri DRAGONS LOVE TACOS

While You Were Napping

The Bear Ate Your Sandwich

It Wasn't Me

Dragons Love Tacos

- "The sandwiches were beautiful pinwheels of color: avocado, tomato and bacon, goat cheese and roasted red pepper, roast beef, cucumber, and horseradish cream."
—Elin Hilderbrand, *The Blue Bistro*, 2005

- "He was just a kid, so I let it go. And now, years later, I probably only think of it, I don't know, once or twice a day."
—Jenny Offill, *Weather*, 2020

- According to the Peanut Advisory Board, by the time the average kid graduates from high school, they will have eaten fifteen hundred peanut butter sandwiches.

- Inventor Thomas Edison claimed to sleep only three to four hours a night, but he kept cots for napping in his office and library, and was often photographed snoozing under trees and in his laboratory. Firsthand accounts say Edison woke from his naps refreshed and alert. In literature, results aren't always so dreamy, as Rip Van Winkle, Gulliver, Sleeping Beauty, and Juliet might attest.

- It wasn't me, it was . . . my pen name. Nora Roberts wrote as J. D. Robb; Anne Brontë as Acton Bell; Agatha Christie as Mary Westmacott; Stephen King as Richard Bachman; Karen Blixen as Isak Dinesen; Eric Arthur Blair as George Orwell; and Amandine Aurore Lucie Dupin as George Sand. Dean Koontz has written under many names: Aaron Wolfe, Anthony North, David Axton, Brian Coffey, John Hill, K. R. Dwyer, Leigh Nichols, and others.

TITLES BY: Jenny Offill and Barry Blitt / Julia Sarcone-Roach / Dana Alison Levy / Adam Rubin and Daniel Salmieri

- "The first step to creating a better world is being able to imagine it."
  —Akwaeke Emezi, "Next Generation Leaders," *Time*, May 27, 2021

- "Fairy tales are more than true: not because they tell us that dragons exist, but because they tell us that dragons can be beaten."
  —Neil Gaiman, *Coraline*, 2002

- "If you have built castles in the air, your work need not be lost; that is where they should be. Now put the foundations under them."
  —Henry David Thoreau, *Walden; or, Life in the Woods*, 1854

- Robert Penn Warren's *All the King's Men* won the 1947 Pulitzer Prize for the Novel. In 1948, the "Novel" category was renamed "Fiction." *All the King's Men* was adapted into two films of the same name, in 1949 and 2006. The 1949 version, directed by Robert Rossen, won three Academy Awards, including Best Picture.

- The popular HBO series *Game of Thrones* was adapted from the series of novels by George R. R. Martin, the first of which is *A Game of Thrones*. Among its many honors, the show received fifty-nine Primetime Emmy Awards, including Outstanding Drama Series from 2015 to 2019.

- The Chinese invented cardboard in the 1600s. In 1817, the English invented the first commercial cardboard box. And in 2005, in Rochester, New York, the cardboard box was inducted into the National Toy Hall of Fame.

Here Be Dragons

Knights vs. Monsters

All the King's Men

A Game of Thrones

Imagine!

Medieval Mayhem

The Cardboard Kingdom

Jack and the Box

TITLES BY: Sharon Kay Penman / Matt Phelan / Robert Penn Warren / George R. R. Martin / Raúl Colón / C. T. Walsh / Chad Sell / Art Spiegelman

 SHARON KAY PENMAN — HERE BE DRAGONS

PHELAN 2 KNIGHTS VS. MONSTERS GREENWILLOW

ALL THE KING'S MEN
ROBERT PENN WARREN

GEORGE R. R. MARTIN A GAME OF THRONES BANTAM

COLÓN IMAGINE! Simon & Sch

MIDDLE SCHOOL MAYHEM: MEDIEVAL MAYHEM C. T. Walsh 5

 CHAD SELL THE CARDBOARD KINGDOM KNOPF

ART SPIEGELMAN JACK AND THE BOX TOON BOOKS

SUCH a FUN AGE k

PICIO Any Day with YOU

Such a Fun Age

Any Day with You

- "If there was ever a more perfect day in the history of time it isn't one I've heard about."
  —Meg Rosoff, *How I Live Now*, 2004

- "I was already the kind of girl who closed my eyes and thumped the backs of furniture looking for hidden doors, and wished on second stars to the right whenever the night was dark enough to see them."
  —Melissa Albert, *The Hazel Wood*, 2018

- "One day spent with someone you love can change everything."
  —Mitch Albom, *For One More Day*, 2006

- "'I wish we had tails to wag,' said Mr. Dearly."
  —Dodie Smith, *The Hundred and One Dalmations*, 1956

- In July 2021, about three hundred years after it was checked out of the Sheffield Cathedral library and two hundred years after the church library was dismantled, a 1704 edition of the 1688 book *The Faith and Practice of a Church of England-Man* found its way back to England. According to *The Star* (Sheffield), the book arrived in the mail with a note from a woman in Wales, whose late godmother had requested its return.

TITLES BY: Kiley Reed / Mae Respicio

- "There should be a song for women to sing at this moment or a prayer to recite. But perhaps there is none because there are no words strong enough to name that moment."
  —Anita Diamant, *The Red Tent*, 1997

- "How can it be, after all this concentrated effort and separation, how can it be that I still resemble, so very closely, my own detestable mother?"
  —Gabrielle Hamilton, *Blood, Bones & Butter: The Inadvertent Education of a Reluctant Chef*, 2001

- The average adult at rest takes between seventeen thousand and twenty-three thousand breaths a day.

- The title of Aldous Huxley's *Brave New World* was taken from Shakespeare's *The Tempest* (act 5, scene 1): "How beauteous mankind is! O brave new world / That has such people in't!"

- German educator Friedrich Froebel coined the word "kindergarten" from the German words *kinder* ("children") and *garten* ("garden") in 1840, when he started the first Garden for Children in Bad Blankenburg, according to Froebel Web. He wrote, "Children are like tiny flowers; they are varied and need care, but each is beautiful alone and glorious when seen in the community of peers."

- Edith Wharton, author of *A Backward Glance*, made history as the first woman to win a Pulitzer Prize, for her 1920 novel, *The Age of Innocence*.

On the First Day of Kindergarten

Butterflies and Moths

Her Own Two Feet

Unsettled Ground

Brave New World

A Backward Glance

A Last Goodbye

There There

Breathe, Mama, Breathe

TITLES BY: Tish Rabe and Laura Hughes / David Carter / Meredith Davis and Rebeka Uwitonze / Claire Fuller / Aldous Huxley / Edith Wharton / Elin Kelsey and Soyeon Kim / Tommy Orange / Shonda Moralis

 Rabe ★ Hughes **On the First Day of Kindergarten** HARPER

 SMITHSONIAN HANDBOOKS **BUTTERFLIES AND MOTHS**

SCHOLASTIC FOCUS **HER OWN TWO FEET**
A RWANDAN GIRL'S BRAVE FIGHT TO WALK · DAVIS UWITONZE

 **Unsettled Ground** **Claire Fuller** TIN HOUSE

P.S. BRAVE NEW WORLD ALDOUS HUXLEY · HARPER PERENNIAL MODERN CLASSICS

Edith Wharton **A BACKWARD GLANCE** TOUCHSTONE SIMON & SCHUSTER

Elin Kelsey **A Last Goodbye** Artwork by Soyeon

 There There *Tommy O*

Moralis **BREATHE, MAMA, BREATHE** THE EXPERIMENT

 are you listening?

TOM RYAN I HOPE YOU'RE LISTENING

ROWE THE WAY I HEARD IT

You're Not Listening | WHAT YOU'RE MISSING AND WHY IT MATTERS | Ka Mur

Are You Listening?

I Hope You're Listening

The Way I Heard It

You're Not Listening

- "Listen. There's something you need to hear."
  —Richard Powers, *The Overstory*, 2018

- "She could see that familiar look on her mom's face. It was her I'm-just-making-conversation-but-really-hoping-you'll-share-something-important look."
  —Celia C. Pérez, *Strange Birds: A Field Guide to Ruffling Feathers*, 2019

- "When a thoughtless or unkind word is spoken, best tune out."
  —Ruth Bader Ginsburg, *My Own Words*, 2016

- A 2021 report by Edison Research and Triton Digital says the percentage of Americans ages twelve and older who say they have ever listened to a podcast is 57 percent, up from 55 percent in 2020.

- In 2007, *The Washington Post* asked world-renowned violinist Joshua Bell to perform during morning rush hour in an arcade outside D.C.'s L'Enfant Plaza Metro station to see if people would stop to listen. Bell put his violin case on the floor, threw in a couple of bucks, and began to play. Pedestrians mostly ignored the virtuoso in the ball cap. In the forty-three minutes he played, Bell made just over thirty-two dollars, including a twenty-dollar bill from a woman who'd been in the audience at a free concert he gave three weeks earlier at the Library of Congress. Gene Weingarten of *The Washington Post* won a 2008 Pulitzer Prize for his feature about the experiment, "Pearls Before Breakfast." In 2014, after a well-publicized effort sponsored in part by the *Post* to promote music education, Bell, in dress clothes and accompanied by nine students from the National YoungArts Foundation, returned to the Metro, this time at Union Station, where Weingarten introduced him. *The Washington Post* headline summed up the second free concert this way: "Joshua Bell's Metro Encore Draws a Crowd."

TITLES BY: Tillie Walden / Tom Ryan / Mike Rowe / Kate Murphy

- "Where were the years? And still."
—Jacqueline Woodson, *Red at the Bone*, 2019

- "Time is the longest distance between two places."
—Tennessee Williams, *The Glass Menagerie*, 1945

- " 'Go,' " she whispered. " 'Go. Show them you spell your name W-O-M-A-N.' "
—Maya Angelou, *Mom & Me & Mom*, 2013

- Dr. Seuss's perennial bestseller *Oh, the Places You'll Go!* was first published in 1990, one year before his death at the age of eighty-seven. In 2004, the American Library Association established the annual Theodor Seuss Geisel Award in his honor to recognize, according to its website, "the most distinguished American book for beginning readers published in English in the United States during the preceding year."

- In 2008, Toni Morrison, Nobel laureate and author of the 1987 Pulitzer Prize–winning *Beloved*, dedicated her first "bench by the road" on Sullivan's Island, South Carolina, to honor the enslaved Africans who were forced to leave their homelands and travel across the Atlantic Ocean. In a 1989 *World* magazine article, Morrison lamented the lack of a memorial: "There's no 300-foot tower, there's no small bench by the road." The plaque on the ground near the bench states, "Nearly half of all African-Americans have ancestors who passed through Sullivan's Island."

- Shortly after Ludwig van Beethoven's death at the age of fifty-six, a friend of the German composer found a letter in a hidden drawer of Beethoven's wardrobe. Called only "Immortal Beloved," the intended recipient of Beethoven's love letter remains unknown.

In the Blink of an Eye

Beloved

Now

Grown

Oh, the Places You'll Go!

Sigh, Gone

TITLES BY: Walter Murch / Toni Morrison / Antoinette Portis / Tiffany D. Jackson / Dr. Seuss / Phuc Tran

IN THE BLINK OF AN EYE 2ND EDITION MU

BELOVED Toni Morriso

tis now

JACKSON  GROWN

Oh, the Places You'll Go!

SIGH, GONE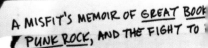

A MISFIT'S MEMOIR OF GREAT BOOK
PUNK ROCK, AND THE FIGHT TO

HEY, KIDDO

Telephone

Love, Mama

Hey, Kiddo

Telephone

Love, Mama

- "All I know is that I carried you for nine months. I fed you, I clothed you, I paid for your college education. Friending me on Facebook seems like a small thing to ask in return."
  —Jodi Picoult, *Sing You Home*, 2011

- "'Now you understand my meaning,' said my mother triumphantly."
  —Amy Tan, *The Joy Luck Club*, 1989

- "He called out for his mother at the end, they all did."
  —Kate Atkinson, *A God in Ruins*, 2015

- At about 122 million, more phone calls are made on Mother's Day than any other day of the year.

- A 2020 Pew Research Center study showed that for the first time since the Great Depression, the majority of young adults— 52 percent of eighteen-to-twenty-nine-year-olds—lived with one or both parents. As coronavirus cases rose, millions of Americans moved in with family. Before 2020, the highest measured value was in 1940, at 48 percent. While the peak may have been higher in the 1930s, there is no data for the period.

- Mother's Day in the United States began in 1868, when Ann Reeves Jarvis established a Mother's Friendship Day to reunite families in West Virginia whose members had fought on opposite sides of the Civil War. Jarvis died in 1905 on the second Sunday in May. Her daughter, Anna Jarvis, memorialized her with a Mother's Day service three years later and, in 1912, trademarked both "Mother's Day" and "the second Sunday in May." In 1914, Woodrow Wilson recognized Mother's Day as a national holiday, using Anna Jarvis's preferred apostrophe placement—the singular possessive—so that each family might honor its singular mother. Years later, Anna felt the holiday had become too commercial and began boycotts and walkouts. She threatened to sue New York's Mother's Day Committee's plans for a large celebration (she won; the event was canceled), and she criticized First Lady Eleanor Roosevelt for using the day to promote charity fundraising. Anna Jarvis died in 1948, penniless from the legal battles to stop the holiday she'd started. She had no children.

TITLES BY: Jarrett J. Krosoczka / Jamey Gambrell and Vladimir Radunsky, after *Telephone* by Kornei Chukovsky / Jeanette Bradley

- "Sometimes I wake up at night in a panic. Wondering: What will my life be like? And sometimes I even wonder: Who am I? What am I doing here, on this planet, in this city, in this house? And it gives me the shivers, makes me panic."
  —Robert Cormier, *Beyond the Chocolate War*, 1985

- "The trouble with having an open mind, of course, is that people will insist on coming along and trying to put things in it."
  —Terry Pratchett, *Diggers*, 1990

- "I've had a sign over my typewriter for over twenty-five years now, which reads 'Don't think!' You must never think at the typewriter—you must feel."
  —Ray Bradbury, *Day at Night*, January 21, 1974

- "Nothing in life is as important as you think it is, while you are thinking about it."
  —Daniel Kahneman, *Thinking, Fast and Slow*, 2011. In 2002, Kahneman and colleague Vernon L. Smith won the Nobel Prize in Economic Sciences "for having integrated insights from psychological research into economic science, especially concerning human judgment and decision-making under uncertainty."

- *Le Penseur*, or *The Thinker*, is one of the most well-known works by French sculptor Auguste Rodin. Designed in 1880 for the tympanum of Rodin's work *The Gates of Hell*, *The Thinker* was originally called *The Poet* after Dante Alighieri, author of *The Divine Comedy*, and inspiration for *The Gates*. Today, casts of the sculpture can be seen in cities across the globe, including Paris, Pasadena, Detroit, Berlin, Buenos Aires, Baltimore, Philadelphia, Moscow, and Kyoto. In 1970, a bomb outside the Cleveland Museum of Art damaged the base and lower legs of the Rodin-supervised cast. To date, *The Thinker* remains there, as is.

Thinking Out Loud

Thinking, Fast and Slow

Thinking Again

Am I Overthinking This?

TITLES BY: Anna Quindlen / Daniel Kahneman / Jan Morris / Michelle Rial

Thinking Out Loud

THINKING,
FAST AND SLOW

Jan Morris *Thinking Again*

RIAL AM I OVERTHINKING THIS? CHRONICLE

DE THE WANDERER

LOOKING TO GET LOST

FINDING A WAY HOME

AI
II
&

The Wanderer

Looking to Get Lost

Finding a Way Home

- "Not all those who wander are lost."
  —J. R. R. Tolkien, *The Fellowship of the Ring*, 1954

- "What good is the brain without traveling shoes?"
  —Rita Dove, "Looking Up from the Page, I Am Reminded of This Mortal Coil," *Collected Poems: 1974–2004*, 2016

- "Walking is mapping with your feet."
  —Lauren Elkin, *Flâneuse: Women Walk the City in Paris, New York, Tokyo, Venice, and London*, 2015

- "Travel far enough, you meet yourself."
  —David Mitchell, *Cloud Atlas*, 2004

- Jessica Bruder's book *Nomadland: Surviving America in the Twenty-First Century* explores how after the Great Recession of the late 2000s, "houseless" Americans traveled around the country looking for seasonal work. The film adapted from the book and directed by Chloé Zhao won the 2021 Academy Awards for Best Picture and Best Director as well as the Best Actress award for Frances McDormand. Zhao made Oscar history as the first woman of color to win Best Director. *Nomadland* was the first Best Picture winner to have premiered via streaming services.

- In October 2021, Merriam-Webster.com added "digital nomad" to their dictionary to describe one who works a job entirely over the internet while traveling, "*especially*: such a person who has no permanent fixed home address."

TITLES BY: Peter Van den Ende / Peter Guralnick / Larry Dane Brimner

- "Like most misery, it started with apparent happiness."
  —Markus Zusak, *The Book Thief*, 2005

- "Have you ever been in love? Horrible, isn't it?"
  —Neil Gaiman, *The Kindly Ones* (The Sandman, Volume 9), 1995

- "The more I know of the world, the more I am convinced that I shall never see a man whom I can really love. I require so much!"
  —Jane Austen, *Sense and Sensibility*, 1811

- "Please, sir, I want some more."
  —Charles Dickens, *Oliver Twist; or, The Parish Boy's Progress*, 1838

- The shortest and oldest word in the English language is "I."

- Bookstore Romance Day, created by independent bookseller Billie Bloebaum in 2019, celebrates "Romance fiction—its books, readers, and writers" on the third Saturday in August. In a 2021 *Fortune* magazine article about the rise in romance fiction readership, particularly over the past year, Bloebaum said she believes "people needed escapism and the guarantee of a happy ending."

Love

Everybody Always

Too Much and Never Enough

TITLES BY: Roddy Doyle / Bob Goff / Mary L. Trump

LOVE RO

EVERYBODY ALWAYS

TOO MUCH AND NEVER ENOUGH M

SO LIGHT, SO HEAVY

S HOLE IN MY LIFE

ALL OF A SUDDEN AND FOREVER HE
OK

So Light, So Heavy

Hole in My Life

All of a Sudden and Forever

[   ]

- "It was not the feeling of completeness I so needed, but the feeling of not being empty."
  —Jonathan Safran Foer, *Everything Is Illuminated*, 2002

- "I said nothing for a time, just ran my fingertips along the edge of the human-shaped emptiness that had been left inside me."
  —Haruki Murakami, *Blind Willow, Sleeping Woman*, 2006

- "Thinking about her was the same as the hole you keep on feeling with your tongue after you lose a tooth. Time after time, my mind kept going to that empty spot, the spot where I felt like she should be."
  —Kate DiCamillo, *Because of Winn-Dixie*, 2000

- "His absence is so big it's like he's there."
  —Patrick Ness, *The Knife of Never Letting Go*, 2008

- Newbery Medal–winning author of *Dead End in Norvelt*, Jack Gantos tells in his 2002 memoir *Hole in My Life* of his "becoming a writer the hard way" after smuggling drugs his last year of high school and spending time in prison.

- *Holes* is Louis Sachar's story of Stanley Yelnats and the curse of his "no-good-dirty-rotten-pig-stealing-great-great-grandfather." With jacket art and design by Vladimir Radunsky, it won the 1999 Newbery Medal and the National Book Award. Sachar also wrote the screenplay for the 2003 film.

TITLES BY: Susanne Strasser / Jack Gantos / Chris Barton and Nicole Xu

PHILOSOPHY

- "I wonder how much of the day I spend just callin' after you."
  —Harper Lee, *To Kill a Mockingbird*, 1960

- "No one tells you how gone gone really is, or how long it lasts."
  —Jandy Nelson, *I'll Give You the Sun*, 2014

- "Thus she returned to the theme of 'before,' but in a different way than she had at first."
  —Elena Ferrante, *My Brilliant Friend*, 2012

- Before the Italian author known as Elena Ferrante became, well, well known, she explained her decision to use a pseudonym in a letter to her publisher. According to a 2020 BBC article about her novel *The Lying Life of Adults*, Ferrante had written: "I believe that books, once they are written, have no need of their authors." In a 2020 interview with *The Guardian* about her favorite books as a young adult, Ferrante said she'd looked first for books with a woman's name in the title. "But the book I read and reread obsessively was *Wuthering Heights*. Today I still find extraordinary the way it describes love, mixing good and bad feelings without any break."

Door

Before After

A House That Once Was

Half of a Yellow Sun

Minus One

TITLES BY: Jihyeon Lee / Anne-Margot Ramstein and Matthias Arégui / Julie Fogliano and Lane Smith / Chimamanda Ngozi Adichie / Doris Iarovici

DOOR

BEFORE AFTER RAMSTEIN &

A HOUSE THAT ONCE WAS

HALF OF A YELLOW SUN
CHIMAMANDA NGOZI ADICHIE

VICI   minus one

JLIAN BARNES The Sense of an Ending VINTAGE

A I P A U L A BEND in THE RIVER VINTAGE

ISE PENNY THE BEAUTIFUL MYSTERY MINOTAUR BOOKS

The WAY OF ALL FLESH by SAMUEL BUTLER

KEMMERER CALL IT WHAT YOU WANT

DOCTOROW & WANG IN REAL LIFE

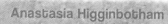 Anastasia Higginbotham DEATH IS STUPID

The Sense of an Ending

A Bend in the River

The Beautiful Mystery

The Way of All Flesh

Call It What You Want

In Real Life

Death Is Stupid

- "You are a person and then you cease to be a person, and a cadaver takes your place."
  —Mary Roach, *Stiff: The Curious Lives of Human Cadavers*, 2003

- "Trap. Horrible trap. At one's birth it is sprung. Some last day must arrive. When you will need to get out of this body. Bad enough. Then we bring a baby here. The terms of the trap are compounded. That baby also must depart. All pleasures should be tainted by that knowledge. But hopeful dear us, we forget. Lord, what is this?"
  —George Saunders, *Lincoln in the Bardo*, 2017

- "You're dead. So how exactly do you live?"
  —Jack Simon, *This Book Is for All Kids, but Especially My Sister Libby. Libby Died*, 2001

- "It *is* heaven, right?"
  —Alice Sebold, *The Lovely Bones*, 2002

- "'It'll always be a mystery,' Dad said, which was no comfort at all."
  —Annie Hartnett, *Rabbit Cake*, 2017

- "I cannot pretend I am without fear. But my predominant feeling is one of gratitude." In the two years before he died from cancer, neurologist and bestselling author Oliver Sacks reflected on his life and imminent death in a series of essays for *The New York Times*. The collection was posthumously published in a 2015 book titled *Gratitude*.

TITLES BY: Julian Barnes / V. S. Naipaul / Louise Penny / Samuel Butler / Brigid Kemmerer / Cory Doctorow and Jen Wang / Anastasia Higginbotham

- "Yesterday's gone on down the river and you can't get it back."
  —Larry McMurtry, *Lonesome Dove*, 1985

- "Yesterday is but today's memory and tomorrow is today's dream."
  —Kahlil Gibran, *The Prophet*, 1923

- "Today is only one day in all the days that will ever be."
  —Ernest Hemingway, *For Whom the Bell Tolls*, 1940

- "I have decided to give the greatest performance of my life! Oh, wait, sorry, that's tomorrow night."
  —Steve Martin, *Born Standing Up: A Comic's Life*, 2007

- The day after tomorrow is called "overmorrow."

- *That Was Now, This Is Then* author Vijay Seshadri won the 2014 Pulitzer Prize for Poetry for his philosophical collection, *3 Sections*.

- According to a May 2021 *Newsweek* article, Cleopatra's reign is closer to our present day than to the building of the Great Pyramid of Giza. Historians estimate the Great Pyramid was built between 2580 BCE and 2560 BCE. The last active pharaoh of ancient Egypt ruled approximately 2,500 years later, from 51 BCE to 30 BCE. "In comparison, her rule was roughly 2,000 years before the first lunar landings in 1969"—and a mere 2,037 years before the first iPhone.

Yesterday Is History

That Was Now, This Is Then

Tomorrow Will Be Different

This Is How It Always Is

TITLES BY: Kosoko Jackson / Vijay Seshadri / Sarah McBride / Laurie Frankel

YESTERDAY is HISTORY

SESHADRI   THAT WAS NOW, THIS IS THEN   GRAYWOL

TOMORROW WILL BE DIFFERENT   SARA

This Is How It Always Is   LA
FRA

NEWS OF THE WORLD PAULETTE JILES

Celeste Ng Little Fires Everywhere

SMOKE AND ASHES **ABIR MUKHERJEE** VINTAG

 SMOKE *and* MIRRORS wm MORROW

The #1 New York Times Bestseller Big Little Lies LIANE MORIARTY B BERKLEY

wow, no thank you. samantha irby

Marconi NEWSMAKERS : Artificial Intelligence and the Future of Journalism

We're Better Than This Elijah Cumm

News of the World

Little Fires Everywhere

Smoke and Ashes

Smoke and Mirrors

Big Little Lies

Wow, No Thank You.

Newsmakers:

We're Better Than This

- "But we must tell our stories, and not be ensnared by them."
—Ta-Nehisi Coates, *The Water Dancer*, 2019

- "People have a right to their own opinions, but not to their own facts."
—James W. Loewen, *Lies My Teacher Told Me: Everything Your American History Textbook Got Wrong*, 1995

- "Lies, my dear boy, are found out immediately, because they are of two sorts. There are lies that have short legs, and lies that have long noses. Your lie, as it happens, is one of those that have a long nose."
—Carlo Collodi, *The Adventures of Pinocchio*, 1883

- "Of course we do have this saying, 'He lies like an eyewitness.'"
—Dmitri Shostakovich, *Testimony: The Memoirs of Dmitri Shostakovich, as Related to and Edited by Solomon Volkov*, 1979. Julian Barnes chose this quote by Russian composer Shostakovich for the epigraph of his 1991 novel about three Londoners, *Talking It Over*. A wife, her husband, and the husband's old friend tell the same story from three different perspectives—their own.

- "Liar, liar! Pants on fire!" So far, origin stories of the playground expression—including one that it came from a poem called "The Liar," attributed to William Blake—have been found to be false, and the creator of the phrase is yet unknown. Linguist Barry Popik says the expression was in use well before the 1920s. A June 2010 entry in etymology blog, *The Big Apple*, notes a version in the February 13, 1922, *Chicago Daily Tribune*, "under the heading 'Do You Remember Way Back When': *We children used to shout: You liar! You liar! Your pants are afire. Your tongue is as long as a telegraph wire.*"

TITLES BY: Paulette Jiles / Celeste Ng / Abir Mukherjee / Neil Gaiman / Liane Moriarty / Samantha Irby / Francesco Marconi / Elijah Cummings with James Dale

- "My life is a perfect graveyard of buried hopes."
  —L. M. Montgomery, *Anne of Green Gables*, 1908

- "But what we call our despair is often only the painful eagerness of unfed hope."
  —George Eliot, *Middlemarch*, 1871

- "It will get easier each time, I think. I hope. I just have to keep trying."
  —Jenny Han, *To All the Boys I've Loved Before*, 2014

- "Because if you grow up to be the kind of person who asks questions about who you are, why things are the way they are, and what we could do to make them better, then you still have hope for this world. And if you still have hope, my love, then so do I."
  —Mira Jacob, *Good Talk: A Memoir in Conversations*, 2018

- The shortest complete sentence (one with a subject and a predicate) in the English language is "I am." The shortest grammatically correct sentence (with an understood subject, "you") is "Go."

A Drop of Hope

Enormous Smallness

TITLES BY: Keith Calabrese / Matthew Burgess and Kris Di Giacomo

A DROP OF HOPE

enormous SMALLNESS

RED D. TAYLOR

ROLL OF THUNDER,
HEAR MY CRY

NA MATA

I PROMISE
I DISSENT

I AM NOT A LABEL

WRITTEN BY

I AM THE STORM

Roll of Thunder, Hear My Cry

I Promise

I Dissent

I Am Not a Label

I Am the Storm

- "Just a regular gal, Jo thought, and smiled, thinking, If you only knew."
  —Jennifer Weiner, *Mrs. Everything*, 2019

- "A well-read woman is a dangerous creature."
  —Lisa Kleypas, *A Wallflower Christmas*, 2008

- "She did things perfectly when enraged. Her eyes focused, her thoughts narrowed, breathing slowed."
  —Louise Erdrich, *The Night Watchman*, 2020

- "Sometimes to kill a dragon, you have to remember that you breathe fire too."
  —Micaiah Johnson, *The Space Between Worlds*, 2020

- Four-time NBA MVP LeBron James, author of *I Promise*, made the cover of *Sports Illustrated* in 2002 as a high school junior. The headline dubbed James "The Chosen One," which James later had tattooed across his shoulder blades. In 2018, he opened I Promise School, a public elementary in Akron, Ohio, for students who, according to the school's website, "are already falling behind and in danger of falling through the cracks." In an April 12, 2019, article in *The New York Times*, James said the school, supported by the LeBron James Family Foundation, is "the coolest thing that I've done in my life thus far," though he credits the school's success to its parents, teachers, and community. The students are called "The Chosen Ones."

- In 2021, Mildred D. Taylor, author of the 1977 Newbery Medal–winning *Roll of Thunder, Hear My Cry* and other honored titles, won the American Library Association's (ALA) Children's Literature Legacy Award for her significant and lasting contributions.

TITLES BY: Mildred D. Taylor / LeBron James and Nina Mata / Debbie Levy and Elizabeth Baddeley / Cerrie Burnell and Lauren Baldo / Jane Yolen, Heidi E. Y. Stemple, and Kristen and Kevin Howdeshell

- "Not everything will be okay, but some things will."
—Ryan Thacker, shared by Maira Kalman at the end of her Creative Mornings talk "Art and the Power of Not Knowing," December 2, 2012

- "Life is unfair, and sometimes it helps to irrationally blame someone for it."
—Michelle Zauner, *Crying in H Mart*, 2021

- "A retreat will teach you again and again that you are neither indispensable nor self-sufficient."
—Karen Lord, *The Best of All Possible Worlds*, 2013

- "One day or day one. / You decide / One bad chapter does not mean it's the end of the / book"
—Paulo Coelho, @paulocoelho, June 13, 2018

- "Love is ridiculous. But love is also wonderful. And powerful."
—Kate DiCamillo, *The Tale of Despereaux*, 2003

- Words born in 2020 quickly became part of the year's global lexicon. Both Merriam-Webster.com and Dictionary.com chose "pandemic" as their Word of the Year. Meanwhile, editors of the *Oxford English Dictionary* "concluded that this is a year which cannot be neatly accommodated in one single word." Among the many in their "Words of an Unprecedented Year" were "lockdown," "social distancing," "doomscrolling," "Zoombombing," "bubble," "systemic racism," "allyship," "Blursday," "Juneteenth," "unmute," and the ever-present "unprecedented."

- According to the Global Language Monitor, the most recognized English-language word on the planet is "OK."

TITLES BY: Fareed Zakaria / Jack Simon / Born This Way Foundation with Lady Gaga / Ozge Samanci / Jason Reynolds and Alexander Nabaum / Maggie Smith / Austin Kleon / Dan Pfeiffer / Lisa Katzenberger and Jaclyn Sinquett / Common / E. Lockhart

Ten Lessons for a Post-Pandemic World

Create Your Culture

Channel Kindness

Dare to Disappoint

Look Both Ways

Keep Moving

Keep Going

Yes We (Still) Can

It Will Be OK

Let Love Have the Last Word

Again Again

TEN LESSONS FOR A POST-PANDEMIC WORLD | FAREED ZAKARIA

NORTON

CREATE YOUR CULTURE | JACK SIMON

BORN THIS WAY FOUNDATION REPORTERS WITH LADY GAGA | CHANNEL KINDNESS
STORIES OF KINDNESS AND COMMUNITY

Samanci | DARE to DISAPPOINT Growing Up in Turkey | FSG

reynolds | LOOK BOTH WAYS

Keep Moving | Maggie Smith

KEEP GOING → • AUSTIN KLEON | workman

YES WE (STILL) CAN | DAN PFEIFFER

 It Will Be Ok | LISA KATZENBERGER — JACLYN SINQUETT

COMMON LET LOVE HAVE THE LAST WORD | ATRIA

e. lockhart | AGAIN AGAIN   DELACORTE PRESS

The List of Things * That Will Not Change

MARY LAURA PHILPOTT  I MISS YOU WHEN I BLINK

BRIELLE NION We're Going to Need More Wine DEY ST.

The List of Things
That Will Not Change

I Miss You When I Blink

We're Going to Need More Wine

- "Wine is bottled poetry." —Erin Morgenstern, *The Night Circus*, 2011

- "As I ate the oysters with their strong taste of the sea and their faint metallic taste that the cold white wine washed away, leaving only the sea taste and the succulent texture, and as I drank their cold liquid from each shell and washed it down with the crisp taste of the wine, I lost the empty feeling and began to be happy and to make plans." —Ernest Hemingway, *A Moveable Feast*, 1964

- "You should always be drunk. . . . But drunk on what? On wine, on poetry, or on virtue, whatever you like. But get yourself drunk." —Charles Baudelaire, *Paris Spleen*, 1869, translated by Raymond N. MacKenzie, 2008

- Mary Laura Philpott, author of the memoir *I Miss You When I Blink*, is a former bookseller at Parnassus in Nashville and was for several years an Emmy-winning cohost of Nashville Public Television's literary interview program *A Word on Words*.

- *A Word on Words* cohost and *New York Times* bestselling author thriller writer J. T. Ellison is a self-described "life-long wine aficionado" who created the website The Wine Vixen to review all varietals and price points. At the time of this writing the website is on hiatus, but as J. T. says there, "It is still full of great wine tips."

- Gabrielle Union, actress, activist, advocate, and author of *We're Going to Need More Wine: Stories That Are Funny, Complicated, and True*, said in a 2017 interview with NPR's Mandalit Del Barco that the stories in her memoir "are helpful with a cocktail, for sure."

TITLES BY: Rebecca Stead / Mary Laura Philpott / Gabrielle Union

- "Have you noticed how nobody ever looks up? Nobody looks at chimneys, or trees against the sky, or the tops of buildings."
—Julie Andrews Edwards, *The Last of the Really Great Whang-doodles*, 1974

- "I felt as if I were in a sound-proof room. Not enough was happening that mattered—that was real."
—Ram Dass, *Be Here Now*, 1971

- "Reality is that which, when you stop believing in it, doesn't go away."
—Philip K. Dick, *I Hope I Shall Arrive Soon*, 1985

- "Reality continues to ruin my life."
—Bill Watterson, "Calvin and Hobbes," *The Complete Calvin and Hobbes*, 2012

- "IRL," whether or not in all caps, means "in real life," as opposed to something happening online, or on a screen on social media, in a game, or on television. "IRL" is not spoken in real life, however. It's used in our digital ones.

- Jennifer Egan's *Look at Me* was a 2001 National Book Awards Finalist. Ten years later, she won the Pulitzer Prize and the National Book Critics Circle Award for *A Visit from the Goon Squad*. In June 2020, reflecting on the book's tenth anniversary in an interview with *Entertainment Weekly*, Egan said that initially the book bombed. Her publisher rushed the paperback printing, and that same month it won the Pulitzer. "It felt like everything changed overnight. We live in a world that cares so much about labels and status. So winning a prize, which is basically a matter of luck in that you have to please the right group of people at the right time, if you get that luck the result is this bizarrely iconic brand association that happens immediately."

5,203 Things to Do Instead of Looking at Your Phone

Look Up!

Look at Me

Be Here Now

IRL

TITLES BY: Barbara Ann Kipfer / Annette LeBlanc Cate / Jennifer Egan / Ram Dass / Chris Stedman

5,203 THINGS TO DO INSTEAD OF LOOKING AT YOUR PHONE

BARBARA ANN KIPFER

workman

ANNETTE LeBLANC CATE   LOOK UP!

LOOK AT ME   a novel   JENNIFER

BE HERE NOW

STEDMAN

Online Dating FOR **DUMMIES**

Infinite Hope

Simon ROBOT BURP HEAD SMARTYPANTS! Candlewi

 you have a match Emma Lord

Online Dating for Dummies

Infinite Hope

Robot Burp Head Smartypants!

You Have a Match

- "It was possible to feel superior to other people and feel like a misfit at the same time."
  —Jeffrey Eugenides, *The Marriage Plot*, 2011

- "I put the questionnaire away. 'Excellent.' I was pleased that my question sequencing was working so well. We could have wasted time talking about ice-cream flavours and make-up only to find that she smoked. Needless to say, smoking was not negotiable. 'No more questions. What would you like to discuss?'"
  —Graeme Simsion, *The Rosie Project*, 2013

- "'Right, and the two of you are just going to hold hands, admire the moon, and sing camp songs.' 'For a while. Minus the singing.'"
  —Nora Roberts, *Savor the Moment*, 2010

- "Don't answer the door in a wedding dress and veil, he might not think you're joking."
  —Amy Sedaris, *I Like You: Hospitality Under the Influence*, 2006

- "It is such a happiness when good people get together." Jane Austen's Emma Woodhouse began her matchmaking 180 years before Match.com launched the world's first online dating website in 1995. *Emma*, published in 1815, has inspired countless retellings and at least four films, including 1995's cult classic *Clueless*, directed by Amy Heckerling and starring Alicia Silverstone and Paul Rudd.

TITLES BY: Judith Silverstein and Michael Lasky / Ashley Bryan / Annette Simon / Emma Lord

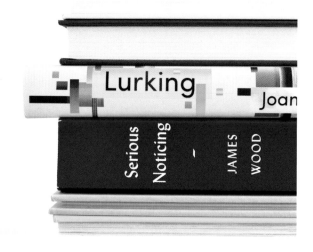

Likes

Temporary

Luster

Lurking

Serious Noticing

TITLES BY: Sarah Shun-Lien Bynum / Hilary Leichter / Raven Leilani

TITLES BY: Joanne McNeil / James Wood

Hashtag

There Must Be More Than That!

No Filter

Let Me Tell You What I Mean

TITLES BY: Elizabeth Losh / Shinsuke Yoshitake

TITLES BY: Sarah Frier / Joan Didion

GEEK LOVE K

Hook Autocomplete: The Boo

WE JUST CLICK

Geek Love

Autocomplete:
We Just Click

- "So now books were her only friends. She'd read *Lord of the Rings* so often she could recite whole scenes by memory. It was not a skill that aided one in becoming popular."
—Kristin Hannah, *Firefly Lane*, 2008

- "'When your mama was the geek, my dreamlets,' Papa would say, 'she made the nipping off of noggins such a crystal mystery that the hens themselves yearned toward her, waltzing around her, hypnotized with longing.'"
—Katherine Dunn, *Geek Love*, 1989

- The word "geek" was first documented in 1916 as a term for circus sideshow performers, whose acts were often called "geek shows." The word came from *geck*, a Low German word for a fool.

- Dr. Seuss introduced the word "nerd" in his book *If I Ran the Zoo* (1950).

- William Gibson has been credited with creating the term "cyberspace" in his 1982 short story "Burning Chrome," after watching kids play video games in arcades. On a legal pad, Gibson scratched out "infospace" and "dataspace" before writing the word "cyberspace." His 1984 novel *Neoromancer* became a cornerstone of the cyberpunk movement. However, in a 2020 interview with *Time* magazine, Gibson said, "Since then I've discovered that a Scandinavian artist previously used [cyberspace] in an abstract painting. Cyberpunk is not my coinage. . . . We were already marginalized as sci-fi writers. Cyberpunk would marginalize us further."

TITLES BY: Katherine Dunn / Justin Hook / Aled Lewis

- "And there followed a strange, elongated couple of minutes."
  —Jojo Moyes, *The Giver of Stars*, 2019

- "I was with family. I was with blood. And I slept."
  —Charlaine Harris, *Dead in the Family*, 2012

- "Goodnight nobody." *Goodnight Moon*, written by Margaret Wise Brown and illustrated by Clement Hurd, has been in print since it was published in 1947. Anne Carroll Moore, an influential children's librarian at the New York Public Library (NYPL), didn't like the book. In a 2020 interview with CBC radio, Betsy Bird, a collections manager at the Evanston Public Library in Illinois who once worked at NYPL, offered an explanation: "[Moore was] a huge fan of Beatrix Potter. She liked a very classic style of children's literature, and when you look at *Goodnight Moon*, it's very glaring." Even after Moore's retirement, it took until 1972 for *Goodnight Moon* to find a home in the NYPL. She still took it upon herself to join meetings. Bird says, "Her successors had her sitting there. If they bought something she didn't particularly like, she was going to tell them in no uncertain terms. So I suspect it kept [*Goodnight Moon*] off the shelves for quite some time." *Goodnight Moon* wasn't the only beloved children's book that didn't pass Moore's muster: she tried to stop publication of E. B. White's *Stuart Little*, and also spurned his 1953 Newbery Honor Medalist, *Charlotte's Web*.

- The framed photograph on the wall of the great green room in *Goodnight Moon* shows a scene from another Brown-Hurd classic: *The Runaway Bunny* (1942). It has also never been out of print.

Hush

Sweet Dreams

Click, Clack, Good Night

Sometimes I Forget You're a Robot

Goodnight iPad

TITLES BY: Dylan Farrow / Jewel and Amy June Bates / Doreen Cronin and Betsy Lewin / Sam Brown / Ann Droyd

HUSH

DYLAN FARROW

WEDNESDAY BOOKS

ATES   SWEET DREAMS   Simon &

EWIN   CLICK, CLACK, GOOD NIGHT

SOMETIMES I FORGET YOU'RE A ROBOT

Ann Droyd   GOODNIGHT iPAD   blue rider press

TEN ARGUMENTS FOR DELETING YOUR
SOCIAL MEDIA ACCOUNTS RIGHT NOW | JARON
LANIER | PICADOR

LAUREN GRAHAM IN CONCLUSION, DON'T WORRY ABOUT IT

YOU ARE NOT A GADGET A Manifesto Jaron Lanier

SAVAGE SIGN OFF

OBERWEGER THANK YOU FOR COMING TO MY TED TALK ◯◇△ HMH

FIND ME André Acimar

AVERBUCH FRIEND ME SCHOLASTIC PRESS

*Ten Arguments for Deleting Your
Social Media Accounts Right Now*

In Conclusion, Don't Worry About It

You Are Not a Gadget

Sign Off

Thank You for Coming to My TED Talk

Find Me

Friend Me

TITLES BY: Jaron Lanier / Lauren Graham / Jaron Lanier / Stephen Savage / Chris Anderson with Lorin Oberweger / André Aciman / Sheila M. Averbuch

- "I was basically born knowing how to casually stalk people on social media."
  —Becky Albertalli, *The Upside of Unrequited*, 2017

- "I can't pretend to understand social media either. I mean, I get it, I just don't understand why so many people spend so much time engaging with it. It's not real. It's just noise."
  —Alice Feeney, *Sometimes I Lie*, 2017

- "I bet you haven't done anything offscreen in months. Have you?"
  —Dave Eggers, *The Circle*, 2013

- According to the Pew Research Center, 70 percent of Americans are active on social media and 25 percent of the country is online "almost constantly."

- Geoffrey Chaucer, author of *The Canterbury Tales*, was the first to use the word "twitter"—in 1392. As tweeted by Oxford English Online (@OED) on October 25, 2012: "#Chaucer provides our earliest ex. of twitter, verb: of a bird: to utter a succession of light tremulous notes; to chirp continuously." Chaucer also coined the words "messagery," "misery," "altercation," "corny," and "snort."

- Facebook's Mark Zuckerberg was not the first person in history to use "friend" as a verb. Law professor and medievalist Sasha Volokh has found examples of use as early as eight hundred years ago, such as:

  "And after soon friended were the King David of Scotland and Stephen, king then of England."
  —Andrew of Wyntoun, *Chronicles*, c. 1425

  "Friend they any, that flatter many?"
  —John Heywood, *Proverbs and Epigrams*, 1562

- In October 2021, Zuckerberg announced Facebook Inc. was changing its name to Meta Platforms Inc., or Meta, for short, to emphasize its focus on the digital "metaverse," a term coined by Neal Stephenson for his 1992 science fiction novel, *Snow Crash*.

- "What she was finding also was how one book led to another, doors kept opening wherever she turned and the days weren't long enough for the reading she wanted to do."
  —Alan Bennett, *The Uncommon Reader*, 2007

- At the start of Queen Victoria's reign (1837–1901), children's books weren't exactly playful. As part of the Sunday School movement, most were designed with a lesson or moral story. But advances in color printing and affordability, the idea of childhood as a developmental stage, and the social acceptance of entertainment led to a new era in books for children. From fairy tales to fantasies, adventures to poetry, and picture books illustrated by artists like Kate Greenaway, Walter Crane, and Randolph Caldecott, the Victorian era brought about the modern children's book.

- The publication of Lewis Carroll's *Alice's Adventures in Wonderland* in 1865 not only firmly established fantasy as part of children's literature, but with the arrival of the internet, it also brought the expression "down the rabbit hole" into popular vernacular. In her *New Yorker* essay "The Rabbit-Hole Rabbit Hole," Kathryn Schulz compared the phrase to Alice's falling in time as well as space. She wrote, "The modern rabbit hole, unlike the original, isn't a means to an end. It's an end in itself—an end without end, inviting us ever onward, urging us to keep becoming, as Alice would say, 'curiouser and curiouser.'"

It

It's a Book

The Victorian Internet

Unplugged Play

TITLES BY: Stephen King / Lane Smith / Tom Standage / Bobbi Conner

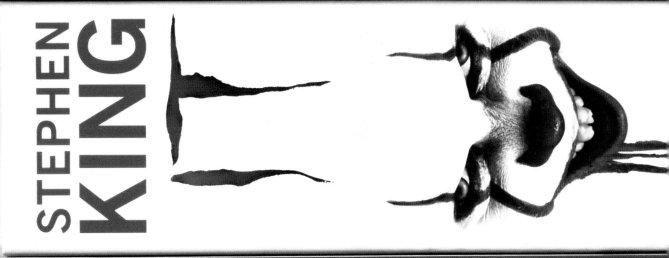

STEPHEN **KING**

TH   IT'S A BOOK

The Victorian Internet   TOM STAND

UNPLUGGED PLAY

CONFESSIONS ON THE 7:45

NEVER HAVE I EVER   JOSHILYN

CAN'T EVEN   Anne Helen Petersen   HMH

 ROSE   May B.   a novel

Confessions on the 7:45

Never Have I Ever

Can't Even

May B.

- "It's impossible to resist the kindness of strangers."
  —Paula Hawkins, *The Girl on the Train*, 2015

- "My first impression was that the stranger's eyes were of an unusually light blue. They met mine for several blank seconds, vacant, unmistakably scared."
  —Christopher Isherwood, *Mr. Norris Changes Trains*, 1933

- "I like to drink when I travel. It enhances things, don't you think?"
  —Patricia Highsmith, *Strangers on a Train*, 1950

- Authors said to have written on the train while on their daily commutes include John le Carré, Jeffery Deaver, and Anthony Trollope, who'd said in *Literary Byways* (1898) that he'd even made himself a tablet to "write as quickly in a railway carriage as I could at my own desk." Agatha Christie brought a typewriter on her beloved train travels. In a letter to her second husband, Max Mallowan, Christie described a 1931 solo trip on the Orient Express, its rain-related delay ("and about 3 a.m. stopped altogether"), and the stories she'd heard of the train becoming stranded in the snow. Her book *Murder on the Orient Express* was published three years later.

- If you'd rather read than write on the train, here are a few books you might track: *The Railway Children* by E. Nesbit (1906), *The Great Railway Bazaar* by Paul Theroux (1975), *Orphan Train* by Christina Baker Kline (2013), and *The Underground Railroad* by Colson Whitehead (2016). For coffee-table beauty, *The Last Steam Railroad in America* by Thomas H. Garver, photographs by O. Winston Link (1995). And for young readers, don't miss *The Little Engine That Could* by Watty Piper, first illustrated by George and Doris Hauman (1930), the 1979 Caldecott Honor book *Freight Train* by Donald Crews, the 1986 Caldecott Medal winner *The Polar Express* by Chris Van Allsburg, *Peacebound Trains* by Haemi Balgassi, illustrated by Chris K. Soentpiet (1996), and the 2014 Caldecott Medal winner, *Locomotive*, by Brian Floca.

TITLES BY: Lisa Unger / Joshilyn Jackson / Anne Helen Petersen / Caroline Starr Rose

- "Careful there, Poet. I might start to believe you."
  —Libba Bray, *The Diviners*, 2012

- "He smiled. 'Now I know how to make you follow me everywhere.'"
  —Madeline Miller, *The Song of Achilles*, 2011

- "There are five dangerous faults which may affect a general: (1) Recklessness, which leads to destruction."
  —Sun Tzu, *The Art of War*, estimated between 475 BCE and 221 BCE

- No one knows the exact date *The Art of War* was written or who the true author is, though it's attributed to Chinese military strategist Sun Tzu, also known as Sunzi. Translated copies of the book found their way from China to Korea and Japan, where it was studied by the samurai. Sometime in the eighteenth century, a Jesuit missionary translated the book into French; Napoleon is said to have been the first Western leader to follow its strategies. *The Art of War* was translated into English in 1905. It became a bestseller in the United States in 2001, when in an episode of HBO's *The Sopranos*, mob boss Tony Soprano told his therapist he'd been reading it. Within two weeks, publisher Oxford University Press had sold all fourteen thousand copies it had in stock and went back to print twenty-five thousand more.

The Way You Make Me Feel

Pretty Reckless

Pretty Tricky

Too Pretty to Be Good

TITLES BY: Maurene Goo / L. J. Shen / Etta Kaner and Ashley Barron / Lindsay Byron

THE WAY YOU MAKE ME FEEL

Pretty RECKLESS

er / Barron

PRETTY TRICKY
THE SNEAKY WAYS PLANTS SURVIVE

TOO PRETTY TO BE GOOD

THIS ISN'T HAPPENING
STEVEN HYDEN

Millan *I Almost Forgot About You* BIDWY

This Isn't Happening

I Almost Forgot About You

- "I've thought about nothing else but you."
  —Iris Murdoch, *The Black Prince*, 1973

- "You are all at once the subject, object, predicate, preposition, and period of my thoughts."
  —Daria Snadowsky, *Anatomy of a Boyfriend*, 2007

- The botanical name of the forget-me-not is myosotis, from the Greek word for "mouse's ear," after the shape of the plant's leaves. The common name of this symbol of remembrance and undying love has several origin stories. German legend says the forget-me-not involved a knight and his love, who'd admired a blue-flowered plant she saw floating in the Danube. The knight jumped in the river to retrieve it but was quickly swept out to sea. He threw her the flowers, shouting *Vergiss mein nicht!*—"Forget me not!" A Greek myth says that after Zeus had finished naming all the plants, a small blue flower shouted, "Forget me not!" Zeus complied. And a Christian story says much the same, though God names the plants. The forget-me-not is Alaska's state flower. In Newfoundland, it honors those killed in World War I. In Armenia, it represents the Armenian Genocide, and for those with Alzheimer's, it's a symbol of hope.

TITLES BY: Steven Hyden / Terry McMillan

- "I'm the evil mastermind behind the scenes. I'm the wicked puppeteer who pulls the strings and makes you dance. I'm your writer."
  —Grant Morrison, *Animal Man* #26, 1990

- "Most writers—poets in especial . . . would positively shudder at letting the public take a peep behind the scenes."
  —Edgar Allan Poe, "The Philosophy of Composition," 1846

- "My mother said I should have a 'change of scenery.' The word *scenery* made me think of a play. And as we were driving around, it made sense that way. Because no matter how much the scenery changed, we were still on the same stage."
  —David Levithan, *Every You, Every Me*, 2011

- Elizabeth Hobbs Keckley, author of *Behind the Scenes, or, Thirty Years a Slave, and Four Years in the White House*, was born enslaved, bought her freedom, and used her dressmaking skills to create a business in Civil War–era Washington, D.C. Keckley designed for Mary Todd Lincoln and the two became friends—until Keckley's 1868 autobiography, which included private correspondence from Mrs. Lincoln. According to Carolyn Sorisio in the *African American Review* 34, the letters were published without Keckley's consent.

- Behind the scenes at *Late Night with David Letterman* was four-time Emmy-winning comedy writer Merrill Markoe, author and artist of the graphic memoir *We Saw Scenery*.

Behind the Scenes

We Saw Scenery

Who Knew?

TITLES BY: Elizabeth Keckley / Merrill Markoe / David Hoffman

BEHIND THE SCENES

The Early Diaries of MERRILL MARKOE

WE SAW SCENERY

MAN

WHO KNEW?

SHELTE
HARBO
PRESS

This Is Just to Say

ell Forgive **Me,** I Meant to Do It

DISCLAIMER A novel

author

TER I Regret Nothing

This Is Just to Say

Forgive Me, I Meant to Do It

Disclaimer

I Regret Nothing

- "What does this say about the life you've lived, then?"
  —André Aciman, *Call Me by Your Name*, 2007

- "At my age, I feel like I'm halfway to the finish line and life's too short to do what I'm sure to hate."
  —Jen Lancaster, *I Regret Nothing: A Memoir*, 2015

- "Maybe all one can do is hope to end up with the right regrets."
  —Arthur Miller, *The Ride Down Mt. Morgan*, 1991

- "Bottom line, wasn't life itself a special occasion?"
  —Jan Karon, *A New Song*, 2000

- According to the website of the American Psychological Association, our biggest regrets don't involve our mistakes, but rather the things we "have failed to do." While "actions cause more pain in the short-term," "inactions are regretted more in the long run," which make us less than the person we might have been.

- A few disclaimers you may have come across:* One size fits all. No purchase necessary. Some assembly required. You must be present to win. Not to be combined with other offers. Void where prohibited. Batteries not included. Do not attempt.
  Participating locations only. Your mileage may vary.

TITLES BY: Joyce Sidman and Pamela Zagarenski / Gail Carson Levine and Matthew Cordell / Renée Knight / Jen Lancaster

- "I'm always interested in products that claim to be aphrodisiacs, when we all know that the one and only aphrodisiac is a man volunteering to build you some bookshelves."
  —Lisa Scottoline and Francesca Serritella, *I Need a Lifeguard Everywhere but the Pool*, 2017

- "My brother and I were able to fantasize far more extravagantly about our parents' tastes and desires, their aspirations and their vices, by scanning their bookcases than by snooping in their closets. Their selves were on their shelves."
  —Anne Fadiman, *Ex Libris: Confessions of a Common Reader*, 2000

- "My books are my brain and my heart made visible."
  —Merilyn Simonds, *Gutenberg's Fingerprint: A Book Lover Bridges the Digital Divide*, 2012

- In April 2020, anonymous Twitter account Bookcase Credibility noted the trend for folks in broadcast to speak in front of their shelves. With the tagline "What you say is not as important as the bookcase behind you," the site probed the bookish backgrounds of politicians and executives, celebrities and CEOs, and not just for titles, but also for plants, framed photos, or lurking cats.

Full Disclosure

I Will Judge You by Your Bookshelf

TITLES BY: Camryn Garrett / Grant Snider

FULL DISCLOSURE CAMI GARRE

I WILL JUDGE YOU BY YOUR BOOKSHELF

R

u v w x y z

Well, That Was Awkward / *Let's Pretend We Never Met* / *Sincerely,* / *Ever Yours* / *The Poet X* / *P.S. I Still Love You*

TITLES BY: Rachel Vail / Melissa Walker / F. S. Yousaf / Vincent van Gogh / Elizabeth Acevedo / Jenny Han

ACKNOWLEDGMENTS

My spine poem of gratitude would topple past Mars.

First: Thank you, Dear Reader.

Also first: To the esteemed authors, artists, editors, and translators whose works grace these pages, I offer my respect, appreciation—and apologies.

Thank you, teachers, librarians, and booksellers, for the magic you perform daily.

Thank you, Rona Brinlee and The BookMark, where the spine poems began, and my Partner in Spine Crime, Pat Underwood Laurence.

Thanks to the team at Harper Design, from publisher Marta Schooler to the folks in contracts, marketing, publicity, and sales. To art director Lynne Yeamans, production director Susan Kosko, copyeditor Jane Cavolina, production editor Suzette Lam. To associate editor Soyolmaa Lkhagvadorj and especially to my editor Elizabeth Sullivan, for her enthusiasm and vision. Thanks to Paul Kepple and Alex Bruce for their beautiful book design.

Thank you, Kathy Shreve Jerrett, for your photo-retouching expertise and lifelong friendship. To Brenda Bowen, I'm beyond grateful for your belief.

Thank you, Dad, for teaching me how to see as an artist, and Mom, for showing me how to fit twenty-eight hours in a day. (Gracefully!) Thanks, Denise, for lending a shoulder and ears. Thanks, June, for your brains, your opinions, your heart. Thank you, Jack, for your confidence that my poems could be a book. And for everything, everything, thank you, Kent.

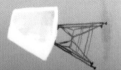

ELEPHANT PIGGIE Book

WE ARE IN A BOOK!

HYP

GROUP

HUG?

We Are in a Book! / Group / Hug?

TITLES BY: Mo Willems / Christie Tate / Charlene Chua

SELECTED BIBLIOGRAPHY

BOOKS

Bernard, André. *Now All We Need Is a Title: Famous Book Titles and How They Got That Way.* New York: W. W. Norton & Company, 1996.

Bird, Betsy, Julie Danielson, and Peter D. Sieruta. *Wild Things! Acts of Mischief in Children's Literature.* Somerville, MA: Candlewick Press, 2014.

Birmingham, Maria, and Josh Holinaty. *A Beginner's Guide to Immortality: From Alchemy to Avatars.* Toronto, ON: Owlkids, 2015.

Burgess, Matthew, with illustrations by Kris Di Giacomo. *Enormous Smallness: A Story of E. E. Cummings.* New York: Enchanted Lion, 2015.

Donovan, Tristan. *It's All a Game: The History of Board Games from Monopoly to Settlers of Catan.* New York: Thomas Dunne Books, 2017.

Gash, Amy, with illustrations by Pierre Le-Tan and foreword by Judith Viorst. *What the Dormouse Said: Lessons for Grown-Ups from Children's Books.* Chapel Hill, NC: Algonquin Books, 1999.

Herrera, Juan Felipe, and Lauren Castillo. *Imagine.* Somerville, MA: Candlewick Press, 2018.

Hoffman, David. *Who Knew? Things You Didn't Know About Things You Know Well.* New York: MJF Books, 2001. Reprint. New York: Shelter Harbor Press, 2016. Citation from the 2016 edition.

Keckley, Elizabeth. *Behind the Scenes: Or, Thirty Years a Slave, and Four Years in the White House.* New York: G. W. Carleton & Co., 1868. Reprinted with an introduction by Dolen Perkins-Valdez. Hillsborough, NC: Eno Publishers, 2016 Citation from the 2016 edition.

McCarthy, Erin (ed.), and the Team at Mental Floss. *The Curious Reader: A Literary Miscellany of Novels & Novelists.* San Rafael, CA: Weldon Owen, 2021.

Moore, Clement. *The Night Before Christmas: or, A Visit from St. Nicholas: The Classic Edition.* 1823. Reprinted with illustrations by Charles Santore. Kennebunkport, ME: Applesauce Press, 2011. Citation from the 2011 edition.

Mount, Jane. *Bibliophile: An Illustrated Miscellany.* San Francisco: Chronicle Books, 2018.

Norris, Mary. *Between You & Me: Confessions of a Comma Queen.* New York: W. W. Norton & Company, 2015.

Williams, Alicia D., and Jacqueline Alcántara. *Jump at the Sun: The True Life Tale of Unstoppable Storycatcher Zora Neale Hurston.* New York: Atheneum/Caitlyn Dlouhy, 2021.

ARTICLES

"The Adoration of the Magi by Leonardo da Vinci, a Unique Masterpiece." Virtual Uffizi Gallery. https://www.virtualuffizi.com/the-adoration-of-the-magi-by-leonardo%2C-a-unique-masterpiece.html.

"Account of a Visit from St. Nicholas." *Troy Sentinel*, December 23, 1823 repro. Troy Public Library, 1998. https://www.merrycoz.org/moore/1823Troy.xhtml.

Adams, Alicia. "We Salute America's Favorite Spread." *Christian Science Monitor*, October 15, 2002. https://www.csmonitor.com/2002/1015/p22s02-hfks.html.

"Adoration of the Magi San Donato in Scopeto." Le Gallerie degli Uffizi. https://www.uffizi.it/en/artworks/adoration-of-the-magi-13fb2318-44ca-4a84-a36d-e41dd12e8181.

"Americans Love Weird Food Combos Like Cookies Dipped in Guacamole, Survey Says." *People*, March 12, 2020. https://people.com/food/americans-love-weird-food-combos-like-cookies-dipped-in-guacamole-survey-says/.

Andrews, Evan. "What Is the Origin of the Heart Symbol?" History.com. February 8, 2016. Updated January 3, 2019. https://www.history.com/news/what-is-the-origin-of-the-heart-symbol.

Anson, Robert Sam. "Clive Davis Fights Back." *Vanity Fair*, February 2, 2000. https://www.vanityfair.com/culture/2000/02/clive-david-bmg-entertainment-ceo-strauss-zelnick.

"Average American Child Asks Parents for a Pet 1,584 Times Before Turning 18, Study Finds." *People*, October 28, 2020. https://people.com/pets/average-child-asks-for-a-pet-1584-times-before-turning-18-study-finds/.

Avey, Tori. "The Caffeinated History of Coffee." The History Kitchen. April 8, 2013. https://www.pbs.org/food/the-history-kitchen/history-coffee/.

Avey, Tori. "Who Was Betty Crocker?" The History Kitchen. February 15, 2013. https://www.pbs.org/food/the-history-kitchen/who-was-betty-crocker/.

"Base Ball Playing—'Defiance' Against 'Sterling.'" *Piqua Democrat*, June 19, 1867. https://www.newspapers.com/clip/56333509/origin-of-dont-judge-a-book-by-its/.

Betty Crocker Kitchens. "The Story of Betty Crocker." BettyCrocker.com. January 10, 2017. https://www.bettycrocker.com/menus-holidays-parties/mhplibrary/parties-and-get-togethers/vintage-betty/the-story-of-betty-crocker.

Biggs, Caroline. "Everything You Need to Know About Forget-Me-Nots." MarthaStewart.com. September 2, 2020. https://www.marthastewart.com/7983151/growing-forget-me-not-flowers.

Bilow, Rochelle. "Meet Tom Iacino, the Man Who Coined the Phrase 'Couch Potato.'" *Bon Appétit*, March 13, 2014. https://www.bonappetit.com/entertaining-style/trends-news/article/tom-iacino-couch-potato.

Bilyeau, Nancy. "Agatha Christie Inspired by Her Own Train Delay to Write 'Murder on the Orient Express.'" Vintage News. January 1, 2018. https://www.thevintagenews.com/2018/01/01/agatha-christie-orient-express/.

Blauvelt, Christian. "Dante and The Divine Comedy: He Took Us on a Tour of Hell." BBC. June 5, 2018. https://www.bbc.com/culture/article/20180604-dante-and-the-divine-comedy-he-took-us-on-a-tour-of-hell.

Boccara, Alice. "Everything You Always Wanted to Know About . . . Mozart's Requiem." France Musique. November 25, 2017. https://www.francemusique.fr/en/everything-you-always-wanted-know-about-mozart-s-requiem-15670.

Bologna, Caroline. "The Weird Backstory Behind Those Valentine's Day Candy Hearts." *Huffington Post*, February 8, 2018. https://www.huffpost.com/entry/history-of-conversation-hearts_n_5a72a8e1e4b06fa61b4d60ef.

Bookcase Credibility. https://twitter.com/bcredibility (accessed August 31, 2021).

Boston Globe. "Hey, If Tony's Reading It, It's Got to Be Good." *Baltimore Sun*, May 13, 2001. https://www.baltimoresun.com/news/bs-xpm-2001-05-13-0105130365-story.html.

Bramen, Lisa. "A History of Western Eating Utensils, from the Scandalous Fork to the Incredible Spork." *Smithsonian*, July 31, 2009. https://www.smithsonianmag.com/arts-culture/a-history-of-western-eating-utensils-from-the-scandalous-fork-to-the-incredible-spork-64593179/.

Brown, Gretchen. "Study: Couples Share Chores More, but Along Gender Lines." Wisconsin Public Radio. April 11, 2018. https://www.wpr.org/study-couples-share-chores-more-along-gender-lines.

Byrnes, Hristina. "22 of the Most Popular Board Games in the US and the History Behind Them." 24/7WallSt.com. April 14, 2021. https://247wallst.com/special-report/2021/04/14/22-of-the-most-popular-board-games-in-the-us-and-the-history-behind-them/6/.

Chrisafis, Angelique. "Proust's Memory-Laden Madeleine Cakes Started Life as Toast, Manuscripts Reveal." *Guardian*, October 19, 2015. https://www.theguardian.com/books/2015/oct/19/proust-madeleine-cakes-started-as-toast-in-search-of-lost-time-manuscripts-reveal.

Clark, Alisson. "Why You Can't Think of That Word on the Tip of Your Tongue—and How to Fix It." University of Florida News. May 31, 2017. https://news.ufl.edu/articles/2017/05/why-you-cant-think-of-that-word-on-the-tip-of-your-tongue--and-how-to-fix-it.html.

Coffey, Laura T. "The History of Mother's Day: The Story of Anna Jarvis." Today.com. May 13, 2017. https://www.today.com/parents/meet-anna-jarvis-founder-fighter-mother-s-day-t110796.

Collister, Lauren. "The Surprisingly Long, Unfunny History of 'LOL.'" *Washington Post*, May 28, 2015. https://www.washingtonpost.com/news/the-intersect/wp/2015/05/28/the-surprisingly-long-and-unfunny-history-of-lol/.

Contrera, Jessica. "Joshua Bell's Metro Encore Draws a Crowd." *Washington Post*, September 30, 2014. https://www.washingtonpost.com/lifestyle/style/joshua-bells-metro-encore-draws-a-crowd/2014/09/30/c28b6c50-48d5-11e4-a046-120a8a855cca_story.html.

"Coquetry." Merriam-Webster.com. https://www.merriam-webster.com/dictionary/coquetry.

"Couch Potato of '90s: Mouse Potato." *Tampa Bay Times*, October 2, 2005. https://www.tampabay.com/archive/1997/10/12/couch-potato-of-90s-mouse-potato/.

Coughlin, Sara. "This Astrological Rule Says Opposites Attract." Refinery29. December 8, 2017. https://www.refinery29.com/en-us/opposite-zodiac-signs-love-compatibility.

Cowles, Gregory. "Oliver Sacks, Neurologist Who Wrote About the Brain's Quirks, Dies at 82." *New York Times*, August 30, 2015. https://www.nytimes.com/2015/08/31/science/oliver-sacks-dies-at-82-neurologist-and-author-explored-the-brains-quirks.html.

Cowley, Malcolm. "F. Scott Fitzgerald Thought This Book Would Be the Best American Novel of His Time." *New Republic*, September 24, 2014. https://newrepublic.com/article/119559/how-f-scott-fitzgerald-wrote-and-revised-tender-night.

Crawford, Amy. "The Surprising Ingenuity Behind 'Goodnight Moon.'" *Smithsonian*, January 26, 2017. https://www.smithsonianmag.com/history/surprising-ingenuity-behind-goodnight-moon-180961923/.

Davidai, Shai, and Thomas Gilgovich. "The Ideal Road Not Taken: The Self-Discrepancies Involved in People's Most Enduring Regrets," *Emotion* 18, no. 3 (2018): 439–52. https://psycnet.apa.org/record/2017-21180-001?doi=1.

Davies, Caroline. "Happy Birthday: How Popular Song Became Public Property." *Guardian*, September 23, 2015. https://www.theguardian.com/business/2015/sep/23/happy-birthday-how-popular-song-became-public-property.

Dawson, Mark. "History of Cardboard Boxes." Confessions of the Professions. https://confessionsoftheprofessions.com/history-cardboard-boxes-infographic/.

Delany, Alex. "What Is Processed Cheese, and Should We Eat It?" Bon Appétit, April 25, 2018. https://www.bonappetit.com/story/what-is-processed-cheese.

Del Barco, Mandalit. "Gabrielle Union Gets Real in 'We're Going to Need More Wine.'" Morning Edition, NPR. October 20, 2017. https://www.npr.org/2017/10/20/558838759/gabrielle-union-gets-real-in-were-going-to-need-more-wine.

De La Roca, Claudia. "Matt Groening Reveals the Location of the Real Springfield." *Smithsonian*, May 2012. https://www.smithsonianmag.com/arts-culture/matt-groening-reveals-the-location-of-the-real-springfield-60583379/.

De León, Concepción. "Having Trouble Finishing This Headline? Then This Article Is for You." *New York Times*, September 6, 2018. https://www.nytimes.com/2018/09/06/books/hyperfocus-chris-bailey-attention-distraction.html.

Diamond, Jared. "Invention Is the Mother of Necessity." *New York Times*, 1999. https://archive.nytimes.com/www.nytimes.com/library/magazine/millennium/m1/diamond.html.

Dietz, Laura. "Trains of Thought: Writing and Commuting." *Guardian*, June 6, 2007. https://www.theguardian.com/books/booksblog/2007/jun/06/trainsofthoughtwritingand.

DiGiacomo, Frank. "Clive Davis Reflects on Janis Joplin's Big Brother & the Holding Company Going No. 1." *Billboard*, September 17, 2019. https://www.billboard.com/articles/columns/rock/8530079/clive-davis-janis-joplin-big-brother-billboard-moment/.

Drye, Willie. "Fountain of Youth." *National Geographic*, January 21, 2017. https://www.nationalgeographic.com/history/article/fountain-of-youth.

Dylan, Bob. "Nobel Lecture." NobelPrize.org. June 5, 2017. https://www.nobelprize.org/prizes/literature/2016/dylan/lecture/.

Eames, Tom. "The Story of . . . 'Imagine' by John Lennon." Smooth Radio. October 8, 2020. https://www.smoothradio.com/features/the-story-of/john-lennon-imagine-lyrics-meaning-facts-video/.

Edmonds, Molly. "Why Is a Tomato Called a Love Apple?" HowStuffWorks. https://recipes.howstuffworks.com/tomato-called-a-love-apple.htm.

"Elvis Defends Low-Down Style." *Charlotte Observer*, June 27, 1956. https://music.arts.uci.edu/abauer/2.1/notes/Music_9_Reader_2020.pdf, 94.

Epstein, Jason. "Food; Chinese Characters." *New York Times Magazine*, June 13, 2004. https://www.nytimes.com/2004/06/13/magazine/food-chinese-characters.html.

Erickson, Alexa. "Here's Why Cats Love Laptops." *Reader's Digest*, July 21, 2021. https://www.rd.com/article/why-cats-love-laptops/.

Eschner, Kat. "The Beloved, Baffling 'A Wrinkle in Time' Was Rejected by 26 Publishers." *Smithsonian*, November 29, 2016. https://www.smithsonianmag.com/smart-news/beloved-baffling-wrinkle-time-was-rejected-26-publishers-180961227/.

Escobar, Natalie. "What Was the Inspiration for 'The Murder on the Orient Express'?" *Smithsonian*, November 22, 2017. https://www.smithsonianmag.com/history/what-was-inspiration-murder-orient-express-180967305/.

Eveleth, Rose. "The History of the Exclamation Point." *Smithsonian*, August 9, 2012. https://www.smithsonianmag.com/smart-news/the-history-of-the-exclamation-point-16445416/.

"Exhibit: Revisiting 'A Visit from St. Nicholas.'" New York State Library. December 2015. https://www.nysl.nysed.gov/collections/stnick/.

"Farmers Stew over 'Couch Potato.'" BBC News. June 20, 2005. http://news.bbc.co.uk/2/hi/uk_news/4108964.stm.

Ferrante, Elena. "Interview: Elena Ferrante: 'We Don't Have to Fear Change, What Is Other Shouldn't Frighten Us.'" *Guardian*, August 29, 2020. https://www.theguardian.com/books/2020/aug/29/elena-ferrante-we-dont-have-to-fear-change-what-is-other-shouldnt-frighten-us.

Ferrell, Nicholas A. "How the Forget-Me-Not Flower Found Its Name." The New Leaf Journal. March 11, 2021. Updated August 6, 2021. https://thenewleafjournal.com/how-the-forget-me-not-flower-found-its-name/.

Finney, Brian. "Irony: Truth's Disguise." *Los Angeles Review of Books*, June 20, 2016. https://lareviewofbooks.org/article/irony-truths-disguise/.

Fish, Tom. "25 History Facts That Will Impress All Your Friends." *Newsweek*, May 26, 2021. https://www.newsweek.com/history-facts-impress-friends-1594925.

Fisher, Jennifer. "The Adventurous Writer Who Brought Nancy Drew to Life." *Smithsonian*, July 2, 2018. https://www.smithsonianmag.com/arts-culture/adventurous-writer-who-brought-Nancy-Drew-to-life-180969479/.

FIVEANDSPICE. "When You Can't Eat Any More, Drink a Digestif." Food52. November 6, 2020. https://food52.com/drinks/14764-when-you-can-t-eat-any-more-drink-a-digestif.

"Flirt." Merriam-Webster.com. https://www.merriam-webster.com/dictionary/flirt.

Fox, Margalit. "Eugene Polley, Conjuror of a Device That Changed TV Habits, Dies at 96." *New York Times*, May 22, 2012. https://www.nytimes.com/2012/05/23/business/eugene-t-polley-inventor-of-the-wireless-tv-remote-dies-at-96.html).

Fraknoi, Andrew. "Light as a Cosmic Time Machine." PBS. March 2008. https://www.pbs.org/seeinginthedark/astronomy-topics/light-as-a-cosmic-time-machine.html.

Franklin, Marc J. "Look Back at over 35 Years of *Cats* on Broadway." *Playbill*, December 20, 2019. https://www.playbill.com/article/look-back-at-over-35-years-of-cats-on-broadway.

"Fred Kroll." *Journal News*, August 7, 2003. https://www.legacy.com/us/obituaries/lohud/name/fred-kroll-obituary?pid=149145558.

Garber, Megan. "'Friend,' as a Verb, Is 800 Years Old." *Atlantic*, July 25, 2013. https://www.theatlantic.com/technology/archive/2013/07/friend-as-a-verb-is-800-years-old/278109/.

Gattuso, Reina. "Why LGBTQ Couples Split Household Tasks More Equally." BBC. March 10, 2021. https://www.bbc.com/worklife/article/20210309-why-lgbtq-couples-split-household-tasks-more-equally.

Gee, Alison. "Who First Said 'The Pen Is Mightier Than the Sword'?" BBC News. January 9, 2015. https://www.bbc.com/news/magazine-30729480.

George, Arthur R. "Coleman Hawkins: Fifty Years Gone, a Saxophone Across Time." All About Jazz. December 12, 2019. https://www.allaboutjazz.com/coleman-hawkins-fifty-years-gone-a-saxophone-across-time-coleman-hawkins.

Gillette, Sam. "*The Hate U Give* Author Angie Thomas Announces New Novel, *Concrete Rose*: 'I Expect It to Get Banned.'" *People*, March 30, 2020. https://people.com/books/the-hate-u-give-author-angie-thomas-announces-new-novel-concrete-rose-i-expect-it-to-get-banned/.

Gleason, David. "The Birth of Top 40 Radio: Todd Storz and KOWH Omaha." World Radio History. https://worldradiohistory.com/KOWH_Birth_of_Top-40.htm.

Goñi, Uki. "Attack of the Giant Rodents or Class War? Argentina's Rich Riled by New Neighbors." *Guardian*, August 22, 2021. https://www.theguardian.com/world/2021/aug/22/argentina-capybaras-giant-rodents-gated-community.

Green, Erica L. "LeBron James Opened a School That Was Considered an Experiment. It's Showing Promise." *New York Times*, April 12, 2019. https://www.nytimes.com/2019/04/12/education/lebron-james-school-ohio.html.

Greene, Andy. "Readers' Poll: The 10 Saddest Songs of All Time." *Rolling Stone*, October 2, 2013. https://www.rollingstone.com/music/music-lists/readers-poll-the-10-saddest-songs-of-all-time-10875/.

Grenby, M. O. "The Origins of Children's Literature." British Library. May 15, 2014. https://www.bl.uk/romantics-and-victorians/articles/the-origins-of-childrens-literature.

Grimes, William. "Milton Glaser, Master Designer of 'I ♥ NY' Logo, Is Dead at 91." *New York Times*, June 28, 2020. https://www.nytimes.com/2020/06/26/obituaries/milton-glaser-dead.html.

Guralnick, Peter. "Dewey Phillips." Memphis Music Hall of Fame. https://memphismusichalloffame.com/inductee/deweyphillips/.

Hamilton, E. L. "The Bizarre Historical Origins of the Humpty Dumpty Nursery Rhyme." Vintage News.com. February 28, 2018. https://www.thevintagenews.com/2018/02/28/humpty-dumpty/.

"'Happy Birthday' Song Officially Recognized in Public Domain." CBS News. June 27, 2016. https://www.cbsnews.com/news/happy-birthday-song-officially-recognized-in-public-domain/.

He, Gu. "Printing." China Today. June 1, 2016. http://www.chinatoday.com.cn/english/culture/2016-06/01/content_721803.htm.

Heisler, Yoni. "Steve Jobs Wasn't a Fan of the Siri Name." Network World. March 28, 2012. https://www.networkworld.com/article/2221246/steve-jobs-wasn-t-a-fan-of-the-siri-name.html.

Hess, Amanda. "The 'Credibility Bookcase' Is the Quarantine's Hottest Accessory." *New York Times*, May 1, 2020. Updated May 22, 2020. https://www.nytimes.com/2020/05/01/arts/quarantine-bookcase-coronavirus.html.

"History of Advertising No 87: The First Ad with Sex Appeal." Campaign. January 16, 2014. https://www.campaignlive.co.uk/article/history-advertising-no-87-first-ad-sex-appeal/1226933.

"The History of Mozart's Requiem." Concert Vienna. June 18, 2019. https://concert-vienna.com/blogs/viennese-things/the-history-of-mozart-s-requiem.

History.com Editors. "The Art of War." History.com. April 23, 2010. Updated August 21, 2018. https://www.history.com/topics/ancient-china/the-art-of-war.

Hook, Paula, and Joe E. Heimlich, revised and adapted by Cynthia Bond. "A History of Packaging." Ohioline. May 11, 2017. https://ohioline.osu.edu/factsheet/cdfs-133.

"I'll Do It Myself." United States Patent and Trademark Office. April 14, 2021. https://www.uspto.gov /learning-and-resources/journeys-innovation /historical-stories/ill-do-it-myself.

Intagliata, Christopher. "The Origin of the Word 'Robot.'" Science Friday. April 22, 2011. https://www.sciencefriday .com/segments/the-origin-of-the-word-robot/.

Jarenwattananon, Patrick. "Coleman Hawkins and Charlie Parker Were Not Particularly Good Actors." A Blog Supreme from NPR Jazz. February 6, 2012. https://www.npr.org/sections/ablogsupreme/ 2012/02/06/146471296/coleman-hawkins-and -charlie-parker-were-not-particularly-good-actors.

Jonze, Spike, and Dave Eggers. "Desperately Seeking Sendak." *Guardian*, November 22, 2009. https://www .theguardian.com/film/2009/nov/22/maurice -sendak-wild-things-jonze.

"Josephine Garis Cochran." National Inventors Hall of Fame. https://www.invent.org/inductees/josephine -garis-cochran.

Kachroo-Levine, Maya. "47 Anthony Bourdain Quotes That Will Inspire You to Travel More, Eat Better, and Enjoy Life." *Travel + Leisure*, February 5, 2019. https:// www.travelandleisure.com/travel-tips/celebrity-travel /anthony-bourdain-travel-food-quotes.

Kane, Jason. "Milky Way." Snack History, August 20, 2021. https://www.snackhistory.com/milky-way.

Kanuckel, Amber. "Forget-Me-Nots: Tips and Symbolism of These Pretty Blue Flowers." Farmers' Almanac. Updated July 13, 2021. https://www .farmersalmanac.com/forget-me-not-blue-flowers.

Kattebelletje. "Stir-Fry: A History." Shared Taste. September 19, 2014. https://sharedtaste .nl/2014/09/19/stir-fry/.

Kessen, David. "Overdue Library Book Returned to Sheffield Cathedral After 300 Years." *Star*. July 9,

2021. https://www.thestar.co.uk/news/people /overdue-library-book-returned-to-sheffield -cathedral-after-300-years-3302790.

Keyser, Hannah. "11 Fascinating Facts About *Goodnight Moon*." Mental Floss. May 18, 2015. https://www .mentalfloss.com/article/64005/11-fascinating-facts -about-goodnight-moon.

King, Rachel. "The Romance Novel Sales Boom Continues." *Fortune*, August 21, 2021. https://fortune .com/2021/08/21/rom-com-pandemic-book-sales -romance-bookstore-day/.

Kingsbury, Margaret. "10 Facts About Madame D'Aulnoy Who Coined the Word Fairytale." Book Riot, March 29, 2021. https://bookriot.com/madame -daulnoy-fairytale-facts.

Kluger, Jeffrey. "Sci-Fi Novelist William Gibson on the Invention of the Term 'Cyberspace' and How AI Could Be Truly Intelligent." *Time*, January 23, 2020. https://time.com/5770124/author-william-gibson -new-book-interview/.

Kois, Dan. "How One Librarian Tried to Squash Goodnight Moon." Slate. January 13, 2020. https:// slate.com/culture/2020/01/goodnight-moon-nypl -10-most-checked-out-books.html.

Kumar, Rita. "An Insight into Weird Cat Behaviors." AmoMedia. August 6, 2020. https://amomedia .com/193163-an-insight-into-weird-cat-behaviors.html.

Lanzendorfer, Joy. "10 Surprising Facts About Mary Shelley's *Frankenstein*." Mental Floss. August 30, 2018. https://www.mentalfloss.com/article/69171/10 -monstrous-facts-about-frankenstein.

Lanzendorfer, Joy. "13 Facts About L. Frank Baum's *Wonderful Wizard of Oz*." Mental Floss. July 28, 2015. https://www.mentalfloss.com/article/66583/13 -facts-about-l-frank-baums-wonderful-wizard-oz.

Le Guin, Ursula K. "The Hand That Rocks the Cradle Writes the Book." *New York Times*, January 22, 1989. https://www.nytimes.com/1989/01/22/books/the -hand-that-rocks-the-cradle-writes-the-book.html.

Lepore, Jill. "Dickens or Bulwer?" *New Yorker*, August 22, 2011. https://www.newyorker.com/books/page -turner/dickens-or-bulwer.

Lepore, Jill. "The Strange and Twisted Life of 'Frankenstein.'" *New Yorker*, February 5, 2018. https:// www.newyorker.com/magazine/2018/02/12/the -strange-and-twisted-life-of-frankenstein.

Lobo, Julius. "The Exclamation Mark! A Brief History!" Book Riot. March 4, 2021. https://bookriot.com /history-of-the-exclamation-mark/.

Lou, Jo. "The 9 Weirdest Naps in Literature." Electric Lit. November 23, 2017. https://electricliterature .com/the-9-weirdest-naps-in-literature/.

Loudis, Jessica. "'Medical' Musing on Politics, Poetry, and Hysteria." NPR. May 26, 2011. https://www.npr .org/2011/07/14/136581522/medical-musing-on -politics-poetry-and-hysteria.

Lowry, Brian. "Academy Awards 2021: 'Nomadland' Wins Best Picture at an Oscars That Spreads the Wealth." CNN Entertainment. April 26, 2021. https://edition .cnn.com/2021/04/25/entertainment/academy -awards-2021/index.html.

Luscombe, Belinda. "Yes, Couples Who Share Chores Have More Sex." *Time*, June 22, 2016. https://time. com/4378502/yes-couples-who-share-chores-have -more-sex/.

MacLellan, Lila. "A New Study on the Psychology of Persistent Regrets Can Teach You How to Live Now." Quartz. June 10, 2018. https://qz.com/work/1298110 /a-new-study-on-the-psychology-of-persistent -regrets-can-teach-you-how-to-live-now/.

Madrigal, Alexis C. "The Rad New Words Added to the Dictionary in the '90s: Where Are They Now?" *Atlantic*, August 28, 2013. https://www.theatlantic.com/technology/archive/2013/08/the-rad-new-words-added-to-the-dictionary-in-the-90s-where-are-they-now/279145/.

"Magnetism." NationalGeographic.org. https://www.nationalgeographic.org/encyclopedia/magnetism/.

Manning, Rich. "Digestifs: What They Are, How They Work, and How They Are Enjoyed." VinePair. May 30, 2021. https://vinepair.com/articles/digestifs-explained/.

Matchar, Emily. "The Pharmacist Who Launched America's Modern Candy Industry." *Smithsonian*, February 8, 2019. https://www.smithsonianmag.com/innovation/pharmacist-who-launched-americas-modern-candy-industry-180971354/.

McDonald, Amy. "Uncola: Seven-Up, Counterculture and the Making of an American Brand." Duke University Libraries. December 4, 2017. https://blogs.library.duke.edu/rubenstein/2017/12/04/uncola/.

McGillis, Roderick. "Children's Literature: Introduction." Oxford Bibliographies. October 25, 2012. Last reviewed April 12, 2019. https://www.oxfordbibliographies.com/view/document/obo-9780199799558/obo-9780199799558-0088.xml.

McHugh, Jess. "How a Single Cookbook Shaped What It Meant to Be an 'American Woman.'" *Literary Hub*. June 2, 2021. https://lithub.com/how-a-single-cookbook-shaped-what-it-meant-to-be-an-american-woman/.

McKinley, Jesse. "'Cats,' Broadway's Longevity Champ, to Close." *New York Times*, February 20, 2000. https://www.nytimes.com/2000/02/20/us/cats-broadway-s-longevity-champ-to-close.html.

McMahon, Kieran. "23.7 Facts About Stanley Kubrick's 'The Shining.'" IndieWire. March 26, 2013. https://www.indiewire.com/2013/03/23-7-facts-about-stanley-kubricks-the-shining-100294/.

McReynolds, Tansee. "Since When Did 'LOL' Become So Not Funny?" Department of Linguistics, University of Colorado Boulder. April 22, 2019. https://www.colorado.edu/linguistics/2019/04/22/inside-guide-everyday-text-talk-evolution-lol.

McRobbie, Linda Rodriguez. "9 Ways *The Art of War* Conquered the World." Mental Floss. May 4, 2015. https://www.mentalfloss.com/article/63366/9-ways-art-war-conquered-world.

Mikkelson, David. "Etymology of 'Oz.'" Snopes. Updated September 30, 2013. https://www.snopes.com/fact-check/the-oz-files/.

Milliot, Jim. "Netflix's Hit Series 'Bridgerton' Drives Book Sales." *Publishers Weekly*, January 22, 2021. https://www.publishersweekly.com/pw/by-topic/industry-news/publisher-news/article/85378-netflix-s-hit-series-bridgerton-drives-book-sales.html.

Moran, Padraig. "Green Eggs and Ham Is 60 Years Old. It Started as a $50 Bet Between Dr. Seuss and His Publisher." CBC Radio. August 14, 2020. https://www.cbc.ca/radio/thecurrent/the-current-for-aug-14-2020-1.5685180/green-eggs-and-ham-is-60-years-old-it-started-as-a-50-bet-between-dr-seuss-and-his-publisher-1.5686697.

Noenickx, Casey. "'Where I'm From': A Crowdsourced Poem That Collects Your Memories of Home." *Morning Edition*, NPR. August 28, 2019. https://www.npr.org/2019/08/28/754698275/where-i-m-from-a-crowdsourced-poem-that-collects-your-memories-of-home.

Nowak, Claire. "Why Do We Use Emojis Anyway? A Fascinating History of Emoticons." *Reader's Digest*, updated May 15, 2019. https://www.rd.com/article/history-of-emoji/.

O'Kane, Caitlin. "Obama's 'A Promised Land' Sells More Than 1.7 Million Copies in Its First Week, Breaking Records." CBS News. November 27, 2020. https://www.cbsnews.com/news/obama-a-promised-land-record-1-7-million-copies.

"'The Partridge Family': THR's 1970 Review." Hollywood Reporter, September 25, 2015. https://www.hollywoodreporter.com/tv/tv-reviews/partridge-family-first-episodes-1970-827360/.

"Pen Names." Writers Write. https://www.writerswrite.com/bookpublishing/pen-names/.

Peterson, Jeff. "What You Probably Didn't Know About Emojis." *Deseret News*, August 2, 2017. Updated August 4, 2017. https://coastalcourier.com/coastal-living/what-you-probably-didnt-know-about-emojis/.

Pope, Conor. "Same-Sex Couples Share Household Chores More Equitably, CSO Finds." *Irish Times*, July 16, 2021. https://www.irishtimes.com/news/ireland/irish-news/same-sex-couples-share-household-chores-more-equitably-cso-finds-1.4622340.

Popik, Barry. "(Liar, Liar) Pants on Fire." The Big Apple. June 2, 2010. https://www.barrypopik.com/index.php/new_york_city/entry/liar_liar_pants_on_fire/.

Popova, Maria. "Thomas Edison, Power-Napper: The Great Inventor on Sleep and Success." The Marginalian. February 11, 2013. https://www.themarginalian.org/2013/02/11/thomas-edison-on-sleep-and-success/.

Quora Contributor. "How Did Siri Get Its Name?" *Forbes*, December 21, 2012. https://www.forbes.com/sites/quora/2012/12/21/how-did-siri-get-its-name/?sh=3ed13e98376b.

Rankin, Seija. "Jennifer Egan on the 10th Anniversary of *A Visit from the Goon Squad* and How It Changed Her Life." *Entertainment Weekly*. https://ew.com/books/jennifer-egan-visit-from-the-goon-squad-10th-anniversary/.

Ray, C. Claiborne. "Q&A: Wild Tomatoes." *New York Times*, July 5, 1994. https://www.nytimes.com/1994/07/05/science/q-a-584371.html.

"Reading 'Can Help Reduce Stress.'" *Telegraph*, March 30, 2009. https://www.telegraph.co.uk/news/health/news/5070874/Reading-can-help-reduce-stress.html.

Rense, Sarah. "Doing the Dishes Is the Chore Most Likely to Kill a Relationship." *Esquire*, April 4, 2018. https://www.esquire.com/lifestyle/sex/a19681230/dirty-dishes-ruins-relationships/.

Rock, David, and Beth Jones. "Why the Typical Performance Review Is Overwhelmingly Biased." *Psychology Today*, May 2, 2018. https://www.psychologytoday.com/us/blog/your-brain-work/201805/why-the-typical-performance-review-is-overwhelmingly-biased.

"Rodin's *The Thinker*." The Cleveland Museum of Art. https://www.clevelandart.org/research/conservation/rodins-thinker.

Rogers, Jude. "Not the Only One: How Yoko Ono Helped Create John Lennon's Imagine." *Guardian*, October 6, 2018. https://www.theguardian.com/culture/2018/oct/06/how-yoko-ono-helped-create-john-lennon-imagine.

Ropper, Allan H, and Brian Burrell. "In Search of Hysteria: The Man Who Thought He Could Define Madness." Literary Hub. September 20, 2019. https://lithub.com/in-search-of-hysteria-the-man-who-thought-he-could-define-madness/.

Rothman, Joshua. "How William Gibson Keeps His Science Fiction Real." *New Yorker*, December 16, 2019. https://www.newyorker.com/magazine/2019/12/16/how-william-gibson-keeps-his-science-fiction-real.

Rushdie, Salman. "Salman Rushdie on Midnight's Children at 40: 'India Is No Longer the Country of This Novel.'" *Guardian*, April 3, 2021. https://www.theguardian.com/books/2021/apr/03/salman-rushdie-on-midnights-children-at-40-india-is-no-longer-the-country-of-this-novel.

Ryzik, Melena. "They Scream! We Scream!" *New York Times*, October 29, 2020. https://www.nytimes.com/2020/10/29/movies/scream-horror.html.

"Saroyan Rejects Pulitzer Prize." *St. Petersburg Times*, May 8, 1940. https://news.google.com/newspapers?nid=888&dat=19400508&id=Z7sKAAAAIBAJ&sjid=Rk0DAAAAIBAJ&pg=5367,2142145.

Schaub, Michael. "Oxford Dictionaries Word of the Year Is an Emoji (Insert Confused Face Emoji Here)." *Los Angeles Times*, November 17, 2015. https://www.latimes.com/books/jacketcopy/la-et-jc-oxford-dictionaries-word-of-the-year-is-an-emoji-20151117-story.html.

Schlosser, Kurt. "Watch Matthew McConaughey Discuss Origin of 'Alright, Alright, Alright.'" Today.com. March 12, 2014. https://www.today.com/popculture/watch-matthew-mcconaughey-discuss-origin-alright-alright-alright-2d79362566 .

Schulz, Kathryn. "The Rabbit-Hole Rabbit Hole." *New Yorker*, June 4, 2015. https://www.newyorker.com/culture/cultural-comment/the-rabbit-hole-rabbit-hole.

Scott, Laurence. "What Ever Happened to the Couch Potato?" *New Yorker*, July 6, 2016. https://www.newyorker.com/tech/annals-of-technology/what-ever-happened-to-the-couch-potato.

Service, Tom. "The Other Where the Wild Things Are." *Guardian*, December 3, 2009. https://www.theguardian.com/music/tomserviceblog/2009/dec/03/where-the-wild-things-are-opera.

"Share the Perspective of Genius." Library of Congress. https://www.loc.gov/exhibits/leonardo/leonardo-exhibit.html.

Shawn, William. "The Postmaster." *New Yorker*, November 13, 1970. https://www.newyorker.com/magazine/1970/11/21/the-postmaster.

Silverman, Leah. "20 Mother's Day Facts to Share with Your Mom." *Town & Country*, May 6, 2020. https://www.townandcountrymag.com/leisure/arts-and-culture/g19561312/mothers-day-facts/.

Simon, Matt. "Fantastically Wrong: The Theory of the Wandering Wombs That Drove Women to Madness." *Wired*, May 7, 2014. https://www.wired.com/2014/05/fantastically-wrong-wandering-womb/.

Skidmore, Chris. "10 Things You Need to Know About the Battle of Bosworth." History Extra. August 22, 2020. https://www.historyextra.com/period/tudor/battle-bosworth-facts-when-where-who-won-richard-iii-henry-vii-tudors-wars-roses-york-lancaster/.

Smith, Laura. "Couch Potato Label Gives Veg a Bad Name—Farmers." *Guardian*, June 19, 2005. https://www.theguardian.com/uk/2005/jun/20/ruralaffairs.foodanddrink.

Snyder, Chris. "Over 100 Hollywood Films Use the Same Scream—Here's How It Became the Go-To Sound Effect for Action Movies." *Business Insider*. November 30, 2018. https://www.businessinsider.com/why-wilhelm-scream-same-sound-effect-hollywood-movies-2018-11.

Sorisio, Carolyn. "Unmasking the Genteel Performer: Elizabeth Keckley's *Behind the Scenes* and the Politics of Public Wrath." *African American Review*, 34, no. 1: 19–38 (2000). https://www.jstor.org/stable/2901182.

Sutton, Robert, and Ben Wigert. "More Harm Than Good: The Truth About Performance Reviews." Gallup. May 6, 2019. https://www.gallup.com/workplace/249332/harm-good-truth-performance-reviews.aspx.

Tanjeem, Namera. "50 Famous Book Titles Taken from Literature." Book Riot. November 14, 2019. https://bookriot.com/book-titles-taken-from-literature/.

"Technological Advances During the Song: Printing." Asia for Educators, Columbia University. http://afe.easia.columbia.edu/songdynasty-module/tech-printing.html.

Temple, Emily. "William Faulkner Was Really Bad at Being a Postman." Literary Hub. September 25, 2018. https://lithub.com/william-faulkner-was-a-really-bad-at-being-a-postman/.

"The Thinker." Musée Rodin. http://www.musee-rodin.fr/en/collections/sculptures/thinker-0.

Thomson, Ian. "The Divine Comedy: The Greatest Single Work of Western Literature." Irish Times, September 8, 2018. https://www.irishtimes.com/culture/books/the-divine-comedy-the-greatest-single-work-of-western-literature-1.3619042.

Thorp, Clare. "The Remarkable Cult of Elena Ferrante." BBC. August 31, 2020. https://www.bbc.com/culture/article/20200828-the-remarkable-cult-of-elena-ferrante.

Tien, Caroline. "Library Book 300 Years Overdue Returned with Note from Woman." Newsweek, July 13, 2021. https://www.newsweek.com/library-book-300-years-overdue-returned-note-woman-1609390.

"Toy Books and Early Modern Picture Books." Children's Books in the Victorian Era from the Winnington-Ingram Collection of Children's Books, International Library of Children's Literature. https://www.kodomo.go.jp/ingram/e/section5/index.html.

Troy, Eric. "Good to the Last Drop: Did Teddy Roosevelt Coin the Slogan for Maxwell House Coffee?" CulinaryLore. September 20, 2013. https://culinarylore.com/drinks:maxwell-house-coffee-and-teddy-roosevelt/.

University of York. "LOL Is Not Just 'Laughing Out Loud'—A New Study Showed That the Function of a Popular Acronym Has Changed." Technology.org. July 27, 2018. https://www.technology.org/2018/07/27/lol-is-not-just-laughing-out-loud-a-new-study-showed-that-the-function-of-a-popular-acronym-has-changed/.

Venn, Lydia. "There's Now an Instagram Account Dedicated to the Duke Licking the Spoon, and Wow." The Tab. January 6, 2021. https://thetab.com/uk/2021/01/06/theres-now-an-instagram-account-dedicated-to-the-duke-licking-the-spoon-and-wow-188292.

"The Wonderful World of Victorian Children's Books." Fine Arts Museums of San Francisco. https://www.famsf.org/blog/wonderful-world-victorian-childrens-books.

"Victorian Illustrators: A Word on Children's Books." Brigham Young University Library. 2021. https://exhibits.lib.byu.edu/victorianillustrators/4.html.

Wee, Rolando Y. "Did Cleopatra Really Live Closer in Time to the First Lunar Landing Than the Great Pyramids?" World Facts, World Atlas. March 13, 2019. https://www.worldatlas.com/articles/so-cleopatra-lived-closer-in-time-to-the-first-lunar-landing-than-the-great-pyramids.html.

Weingarten, Gene. "Pearls Before Breakfast: Can One of the Nation's Great Musicians Cut Through the Fog of a D.C. Rush Hour? Let's Find Out." Washington Post, April 8, 2007. https://www.washingtonpost.com/lifestyle/magazine/pearls-before-breakfast-can-one-of-the-nations-great-musicians-cut-through-the-fog-of-a-dc-rush-hour-lets-find-out/2014/09/23/8a6d46da-4331-11e4-b47c-f5889e061e5f_story.html.

Weingarten, Gene. "Setting the Record Straight on the Joshua Bell Experiment." Washington Post, October 14, 2014. https://www.washingtonpost.com/news/style/wp/2014/10/14/gene-weingarten-setting-the-record-straight-on-the-joshua-bell-experiment/.

Wenk, Gary. "Why Does Coffee Make Us Feel So Good?" Psychology Today, October 28, 2011. https://www.psychologytoday.com/us/blog/your-brain-food/201110/why-does-coffee-make-us-feel-so-good.

Wilson, Robert. "Two New Lives of Harry Houdini." Wall Street Journal, March 13, 2020. https://www.wsj.com/articles/two-new-lives-of-harry-houdini-11584113644.

Wolfson, Andrew. "Who Really Wrote the 'Happy Birthday' Song?" Courier-Journal (Louisville). June 29, 2013. https://www.usatoday.com/story/news/nation/2013/06/29/who-really-wrote-the-happy-birthday-song-/2475837/.

Yorio, Kara. "A Grateful Michaela Goade Makes Caldecott History." School Library Journal, January 25, 2021. https://www.slj.com/?detailStory=grateful-michaela-goade-makes-caldecott-history-2021-youth-media-awards.

WEBSITES

ala.org

bannedbooksweek.org

billboard.com

bookriot.com

bookshop.org

brianjayjones.com

britannica.com

dictionary.com

emojipedia.org

etymonline.com

froebelweb.org

gallup.com

georgeellalyon.com

goodreads.com

guinnessworldrecords.com

harpercollins.com

helenfisher.com

hillaryjordan.com

imdb.com

ipromise.school

languagemonitor.com

lettersofnote.com

lithub.com

maxbrooks.com

nationalbook.org

nationalgeographic.com

nationalgeographic.org

npr.org

oed.com

pbs.org

pen.org

pewresearch.org

phrases.org

poetryfoundation.org

poets.org

pulitzer.org

quoteinvestigator.com

reference.com/science

savinghappybirthday.com

sunrecords.com

themarginalian.org

toyhalloffame.org/toys/cardboard-box

uselessetymology.com

vocabulary.com/dictionary

wikipedia.org

williamsaroyanfoundation.org

wonderstruckthebook.com

worldradiohistory.com

youngarts.org

VIDEO

"Day at Night: Ray Bradbury." YouTube video, 29:04. Posted by CUNY TV, March 11, 2011. https://www.youtube.com/watch?v=tTXckvj7KL4&ab_channel=CUNYTV.

"Maira Kalman: Art and the Power of Not Knowing." YouTube video, 21:20. Posted by CreativeMornings HQ, December 2, 2012. https://www.youtube.com/watch?v=n3TEeUNXxpM&ab_channel=CreativeMorningsHQ

RADIO

"Simon Wrote Songs for Classic Film." *Fresh Air with Terry Gross*. NPR. December 11, 2000.

"Why Goodnight Moon Didn't Make New York Public Library's List of Most Checked-Out Books." *As It Happens*. CBC Radio. January 15, 2020.

HarperCollins books may be purchased for educational, business,
or sales promotional use. For information, please e-mail the
Special Markets Department at SPsales@harpercollins.com.

First published in 2022 by
Harper Design
An Imprint of HarperCollins *Publishers*
195 Broadway
New York, NY 10007
Tel: (212) 207-7000
Fax: (855) 746-6023

harperdesign@harpercollins.com
www.hc.com

Distributed throughout the world by
HarperCollins *Publishers*
195 Broadway
New York, NY 10007

ISBN 978-0-06-320822-3
Library of Congress Control Number: 2021040229

Photographs by Annette Dauphin Simon

Book design by Paul Kepple and Alex Bruce at Headcase Design
www.headcasedesign.com

Printed in Malaysia

First Printing, 2022

One Last Word

Mic Drop

TITLES BY: Nikki Grimes / Sharna Jackson

ES ONE LAST WORD

MIC DROP A HIG
MYS

ABOUT THE AUTHOR

Annette Dauphin Simon is the author and illustrator of several books for young readers, including *Mocking Birdies* and *Robot Zombie Frankenstein!* A former advertising creative director, she first found spine poetry—or spine poetry found her—as a bookseller in an independent bookshop. A proud parent of two lovely grown humans and one who lives yet in her heart, Annette's at home in Southport, North Carolina. And any place with a book.

Please visit her online at annettesimon.net.